TRAINING
SOURCES

Facilitating Learning

TRAINING
SOURCES

Facilitating Learning

book of activities

TONY SPINKS
PHIL CLEMENTS

Viva Books

New Delhi | Mumbai | Chennai | Kolkata | Bangalore | Hyderabad | Kochi | Guwahati

First published as "Training Activities: Facilitating Learning"

This edition published in 2009
Reprinted 2010

VIVA BOOKS PRIVATE LIMITED

- 4737/23 Ansari Road, Daryaganj, New Delhi 110 002
  E-mail: vivadelhi@vivagroupindia.net, Tel. 42242200
- 76, Service Industries, Shirvane, Sector 1, Nerul, Navi Mumbai 400 706
  E-mail: vivamumbai@vivagroupindia.net, Tel. 27721273, 27721274
- Jamals Fazal Chambers, 26 Greams Road, Chennai 600 006
  E-mail: vivachennai@vivagroupindia.net, Tel. 28290304, 28294241
- B-103, Jindal Towers, 21/1A/3 Darga Road, Kolkata 700 017
  E-mail: vivakolkata@vivagroupindia.net, Tel. 22836381, 22816713
- 7, Sovereign Park Apartments, 56-58, K. R. Road, Basavanagudi, Bangalore 560 004
  E-mail: vivabangalore@vivagroupindia.net, Tel. 26607409, 26607410
- 101-102 Mughal Marc Apartments, 3-4-637 to 641, Narayanguda, Hyderabad 500 029
  E-mail: vivahyderabad@vivagroupindia.net, Tel. 27564481, 27564482
- Beevi Towers, First Floor, SRM Road, Kaloor, Kochi 682 018, Kerala
  E-mail: vivakochi@vivagroupindia.net, Tel: 0484-2403055, 2403056
- 232, GNB Road, Beside UCO Bank, Silpukhuri, Guwahati - 781 003
  E-mail: vivaguwahati@vivagroupindia.net, Tel: 0361-2666386

www.vivagroupindia.com

Published by arrangement with

Kogan Page Limited
120 Pentonville Road
London, N1 9JN, UK

ISBN-10: 81-309-1058-6
ISBN-13: 978-81-309-1058-1

Published by Vinod Vasishtha for Viva Books Private Limited, 4737/23, Ansari Road, New Delhi-110 002. Printed and bound by Raj Press, R-3, Inderpuri, New Delhi - 110 012

CONTENTS

Acknowledgements

This book, as with the others we have written, would not have been possible without the help and support of our publisher Kogan Page and in particular Dolores Black. I would also like to mention my good friends Ralph Withers, who has proven a continuing influence on my thinking about effective facilitation, and Chris Moore who always encourages me to think beyond my immediate experience.

T.S.

My thinking about facilitation activities has largely been influenced by having my own learning facilitated by excellent professionals. Among others I am indebted to Diana Yach, Meg Bond, James Kilty, Randall Metzger, John Jones, Mike Eales, Anouk Grave, Mike Spraggon and Robin Oakley who, over the years, have played a greater part than they know in my learning. Writing as a spare time occupation inevitably disrupts family life more than I would wish, and as always thanks go to Heather, Tom and Matthew for their patience and understanding.

P.C.

All the exercises in this book are our own. They have been developed over a number of years of working with hundreds of students, and have all been tested. We ourselves have also been learners on facilitated courses and inevitably we have come away with ideas from which some of the exercises in this book have developed. We have used no source material other than our own notes for the 50 exercises we include. If there is any similarity with other facilitated exercises you may have come across, we apologize and hope that our offerings may give a different perspective and take the process a little further.

T.S. and P.C.

Part I

Choosing and Using Learning Activities and Exercises

INTRODUCTION

Facilitation is primarily about enabling, supporting and encouraging student learning. This is achieved by adopting a flexible style of teaching which is student-centred, experiential and activity-based.

But providing students with a variety of interesting activities that offer relevant and appropriate learning experiences isn't always easy. Until now, the type of facilitation exercises that have been offered have tended to be inflexible, requiring the trainer to adopt the material as it is set out, with little scope for alteration or amendment. As a result, courses often have to be tailored to accommodate the exercises and activities that are available and these, in turn, then tend to drive course design rather than complement and strengthen it. An important consequence of this has been that students find themselves with little input into a learning process whose agenda seems fixed and unresponsive to their needs.

This book overcomes this problem by providing a rich variety of facilitative exercises and activities for all stages of a training course, designed from the outset to be flexible and transferable from one learning environment to another.

Rather than launch straight into the exercises and activities themselves, this book also offers important guidance regarding some of the key issues concerning the choice and use of exercises and activities in facilitated training. It takes care to consider questions such as when to employ exercises and how to draw out learning through effective feedback. There is also specific information about the nature and use of core exercises and the benefits to be gained from them.

Apart from offering a variety of ice-breakers, energizers and course-closure activities, there are also three large simulations and 34 exercises which encourage learners to be open about their feelings and attitudes. These have been designed to encourage and facilitate both the identification and sharing of relevant learner issues, problems and experiences as well as supporting structured reflection and review of what has been uncovered.

This lively and accessible book will prove a valuable resource to all those who are offering, or who plan to offer, facilitated training courses, whether in-house or on a freelance basis. In addition, it will prove useful to trainers engaged in staff development training, as well as to those starting out in facilitation for the first time. The exercises have broad application and should prove relevant in a variety of fields, including equal opportunities training, interpersonal skills training, management training, assertiveness training and quality of service training.

So whether you are an established facilitator searching for fresh and dynamic ideas, a training manager seeking to enhance your available resources, or a new facilitator looking for ways to encourage relevant and meaningful learning for your trainees, this book has a lot to offer you. We hope you will find it useful, useable and resourceful.

CHAPTER 1

How to use the book

We have designed the book to be as easy to use as possible. Remember also that you may photocopy the activities pages to use when you run the exercises.

After you have read this chapter we hope you will have a good idea of:

- Some of the terms we have used.
- The assumptions we have made about you, the reader and user of the exercises.
- How to access the exercises you want.
- What you can expect to find in the layout for each exercise.

TERMS WE HAVE USED

In order to make the book have as wide an application as possible we have not restricted ourselves to using words and labels which limit the exercises to a particular form of training. You can use these exercises in many contexts, so for example you will see the words 'course', 'session', 'seminar', 'training event', which all refer to the time when training takes place, be it one hour, one day or in the context of a whole term's work.

Additionally, we have employed a variety of descriptions of the people doing the training. So we refer to learner, participant, student to reflect that in your different context these people will inevitably be called different things. In mainstream education, for example, 'student' or 'learner' is the most likely; in vocational training, 'delegate' or 'participant' is quite common.

ASSUMPTIONS WE HAVE MADE ABOUT YOU THE READER

We have assumed throughout two main things:

1. That you have at least some experience of facilitation, or at least are in the process of learning how to facilitate. All the exercises in the book are what we call 'set pieces'. This means that they are pre-prepared, and will be built into your wider plan for the training. We are assuming that you are familiar with the general facilitative techniques of group work, defining, discussing, brainstorming, reflecting questions back and so on. All these techniques are fully described and discussed in *A Practical Guide to Facilitation Skills* (Spinks and Clements, 1993, published by Kogan Page). While the exercises give you all you need to know to run them, they still need the application of facilitator skill that you will bring to them.
2. We are also assuming that you have a good knowledge of the content of what you are training. There is a school of thought which suggests that facilitators don't need to know about the subject they are facilitating. They remain neutral and don't have any involvement in the content. Apart from some very limited applications of facilitation we do not subscribe to this view. What this means is that if you have selected an exercise such as 'Selections', which has management and equal opportunities application, we are expecting that you will have a good working knowledge of the Equal Opportunities Commission's guidelines on fair and efficient selection.

ACCESSING THE EXERCISES YOU WANT

There are 50 exercises, listed alphabetically by title, to choose from and there are several ways to access what you want. You will find two matrices which list them at the back of the book.

- by type of exercise, eg, ice-breaker,
- by suggested application, eg, quality of service training,
- by title and number.

Note that the suggested type of exercise and its application are not meant to be set in stone. Virtually all the exercises are adaptable for other uses. How much you adapt them and for what purpose is really only limited by your skill and imagination.

HOW EACH EXERCISE IS LAID OUT

Each of the exercises follows the same pattern of layout to make them easier to use. In the following section we give that layout with some notes under each heading which you may find useful.

Title

The title for each exercise gives an idea of what the exercise is about and provides a reference point for accessing them.

Time guide

The time we have indicated is based on our experience of how long the exercise should take. Please bear in mind that it is a very rough guide to help you with your planning; in reality, the length of time an exercise takes will vary. How willing your group is to discuss (or your skill at facilitating discussion) will be a primary factor in determining the time taken, as will the number of participants in the group. With exercises such as the Round Robin, remember that you need to multiply the anticipated length of time each learner will be given to speak by the number of students. It can often be surprising how much time is used up. Deciding whether to cut a discussion short is really a matter of judgement, but as a rule it is probably best to let the discussion flow provided it is keeping to the aim of the exercise and is still producing meaningful disclosure (see Chapter 3) and significant learning.

Participants

You will need to be flexible about this because in a sense you are stuck with the number of people you have and there will often be nothing you can do about it. If you do have control over numbers however, we have found 15 to be a very good number to work with, enabling effective small group work, distributing the pressure on participants evenly.

Equipment and resources

Where you see the word 'flipchart' we mean A1-sized paper sheets. Broad nibbed pens are the most suitable for writing on flipcharts. The type you can buy for writing on whiteboards work well. Remember to brief the writers that the lettering they use will need to be large enough for the whole group to see: this is the whole point in using a flipchart. A quick demonstration from you is good practice. To stick a flipchart on the board or wall, it is best to use masking tape, which while very sticky, does not damage surfaces when you remove it.

We have indicated where you will need a photocopy of the resource page. In some cases we recommend you cut the sheet up and stick the various categories onto card. This makes them easier to distribute, much more durable for the learners, and you can reuse them another time.

Many of the exercises and activities include resource pages. These pages are part and parcel of the exercise to which they relate and provide all of the documentation you require to run the exercise effectively. Resource pages may be photocopied freely for use in your training sessions (but see the rider on the copyright page).

Application

Equal opportunities training
Interpersonal skills training
Management training
Staff development training
Assertiveness training
Quality of service training

While we have given an indication of the areas where we feel the exercise would be a useful tool, these are not set in stone and you will wish to use your own judgement about the area in which you want to use the exercise.

Category

Ice-breaker

As the name implies, these exercises help students to get to know each other and get used to the idea of opening up in discussion. They are an essential precursor to most facilitated training.

Energizer

Designed as mid-session reviews, or exercises to get energy levels of the group back up to an effective level, energizers play an important role after breaks. Early afternoon after lunch is often a time when they are needed.

Simulation and/or role play

These exercises recreate some aspect of reality, and in safe conditions allow participants to work through real-world issues and problems. Together with the next category of exercise, they lie at the core of learner development through facilitation.

Encouraging learning through openness (attitudes, feelings)

These exercises will stimulate purposeful discussion and help individuals work through their own thoughts and feelings about particular issues.

Course closure

Learning from a facilitated course should never be left in a vacuum but be put in the context of the learner's real world. Course closure exercises will help learners both to do this and plan to apply their learning to their own context.

Aim

This is a broad statement of where the exercise will take you. It will need to be communicated to the participants at the outset.

Issues raised by this exercise

We cannot pretend that we have covered every possibility in this section but you should get a good idea of the types of issue that you can expect to come up and need discussion. It is likely that you will find other issues that the exercise will raise, and in fact we would encourage you to do so.

Method

Detailed instructions are given about running each exercise. Remember to always start by giving a clear aim, so that learners do not think you are being devious or, even worse, setting them up.

Variations

If there is a suitable way of running the exercise differently or making it particularly suitable for a different application we have shown this here. Not all exercises offer a variation but, as always, you may seek to make your own variations.

Feedback advice

Chapter 3 discusses some of the issues relating to feedback and the advice we offer in this section of the exercise layout assumes that you have read it. Having said that, we offer some advice about getting the most from the exercise and also, where appropriate, give examples of questions you might use to get things started and achieve some depth.

CHAPTER 2

HOW TO CHOOSE AND RUN THE EXERCISES

OUTLINE

Facilitation requires the enabling of student learning through guidance and support and the choice and use of learning exercises should serve to enhance this approach, adding to the total learning experience and offering students a vehicle by which experiential learning becomes both possible and successful. This chapter will consider some of the issues surrounding learning exercises and activities, offering guidance and advice along the way.

By the time you have finished reading this chapter we anticipate that:

- You will understand the distinction between learning exercises and learning activities and why this distinction is important.
- You will have considered some of the positive and negative reasons why learning exercises are chosen.
- You will have a better understanding of how to avoid choosing and using exercises for the wrong reasons.
- You will have a greater awareness of the ways in which exercises can be used to promote effective student learning.
- You will have thought about ice-breakers and energizers.
- You will understand what we mean by the term 'core exercises' and their importance to relevant and meaningful learning for your students.

LEARNING EXERCISES AND LEARNING ACTIVITIES

Within any facilitated learning course it is likely that you will make use of a diverse array of facilitative methods in order to effectively structure unfolding learning and, through changes in the way you work with the group and encourage them to work with each other, maintain group momentum and keep levels of interest high.

This diversity of approach should include your choice and use of learning exercises and activities; but what is the distinction between exercises and activities? We would characterize learning activities as those ways of working with the group which are not preplanned but are spontaneous and responsive to immediate learning need. Examples might include:

- spontaneous brainstorming
- unplanned small group discussion
- on-the-spot role play
- quick input by the facilitator (to explain a model which illustrates the point being discussed, for example)
- a 'round-robin' type activity whereby each student takes it in turn to give their thoughts on or react to a given issue or learning point.

In contrast, learning exercises, including those in this binder, are characterized by an element of preplanning and may require materials. Typically they have a set timescale and are designed to bring out specific learning or provide specific learning experiences. They come with pre-defined learning intentions or an attached aim and are structured, often with fixed phases which build one upon another in a developmental process. Examples of learning exercises might include:

- preplanned role-play
- structured simulation of a real-world event or scenario
- case studies
- structured problem-solving
- published 'off-the-peg' exercises (such as those provided here).

It is important to stress that both learning activities and learning exercises are useful facilitative tools which, when used effectively, can serve to maximize learning for your students. It would be senseless to suggest that learning exercises, by their planned and structured nature, are a better facilitative tool than learning activities or vice versa. However, it can be seen that, by virtue of their different form, each can be used to best effect only when they become aligned with points during the course when their use fits best with the learning process at that stage. For example, when the thoughts of learners are flowing and group learning momentum and interest levels are high, it is often better to utilize the more spontaneous learning activity than to interrupt the flow with an exercise which requires explanatory briefing and possibly a change of focus.

NEGATIVE AND POSITIVE REASONS FOR CHOOSING TO USE AN EXERCISE

At the planning stage of any facilitative course it is all too easy to fill in timetable slots with learning exercises which, because they are often a known quantity, having been run by the facilitator on previous occasions, and by virtue of their relatively fixed duration, offer an easy solution to the problem of how to structure learning events.

We have spoken to many facilitators about their choice and use of certain exercises and have found plenty of similarities in their responses: 'I like this exercise, it's easy (or straightforward) to run' or, 'The students like the exercise and seem to have good fun doing it'. Alternatively, facilitators cite the fact that they need something to fill-up that problematic 45-minute slot or they favour exercises which last about 45–60 minutes because they fit nicely between coffee and lunch!

Unfortunately, we have seen little evidence of a systematic and planned developmental utilization of exercises based upon anticipated learning outcomes. The ideal situation is clearly one in which the facilitator, with knowledge of a wide array of learning exercises, carefully considers their appropriateness and relevance to student learning needs at various key stages of the course.

In addition, exercises do not simply become shoe-horned into available slots but instead become earmarked as potentially suitable and are kept in hand, ready for use if and when need dictates. In this scenario the facilitator would take several potential exercises along for each key learning phase, deciding which is the more suitable at the point of course delivery, thus approaching learning with a more flexible and responsive course plan.

When deciding whether a particular exercise should be utilized at a particular learning stage, the facilitator should consider the potential learning outcomes that the exercise offers and any variations to its design which might allow an otherwise non-relevant exercise to become amended sufficiently for it to offer relevant learning. We have listed below a rough-and-ready set of examples from our own experience which, while clearly not definitive, will give you an idea of elements you might consider when evaluating an exercise or group of exercises.

- The exercise is designed to build or clarify a learning agenda or generate ground rules and can thus be used at points during a course where these elements are important or arise.
- The exercise is designed to generate new ideas. These can often be useful at the outset of a new learning phase where the facilitator needs to generate new material on a given issue to work through with the group.
- The exercise offers a means of dealing with conflict which has arisen within the group or is raised as a real-world problem which a student asks to be considered by the group.
- The exercise provides a non-threatening means of encouraging student disclosure on a given subject. Such exercises can prove immensely useful at stages on a course when the facilitator needs to encourage students to begin dealing with their own opinions, attitudes, values and beliefs as a means of fostering appropriate personal development and change.
- The exercise is one which encourages greater learner autonomy and student-centred learning, allowing the focus to move away from facilitator-led phases.
- The exercise offers a distinct change of pace to the flow of learning, allowing the facilitator to better manage attention and interest levels and keep group momentum and motivation high.
- The exercise increases group ownership of the learning taking place and allows the focus to shift from facilitator-led to student-led forms of learning.
- The exercise is designed to meet a specific temporal course need, such as course closure exercises.
- The exercise is particularly good at encouraging student participation and would be most useful when group or individual participation is felt to be a problem or in need of encouragement.
- The exercise serves to illustrate a specific learning point and is the most appropriate means of doing so in the circumstances, having given consideration to such elements as group momentum and levels of interest as well as timescales.

- The exercise offers a good way of linking an unknown topic area with the known in the form of the students' existing experiences and knowledge.
- The exercise is designed as an ice-breaker and would clearly find use at the outset of a course when there is a need for group members to get to know each other and relax within the learning environment.
- The exercise is designed to promote experiential learning by creating a structured learning experience which often has links with real-world issues and problems.

UNDERSTANDING POSSIBLE DANGERS INHERENT IN EXERCISES

Carefully considering the applicability and fit of a particular exercise to the overall course plan is important, but it is not the whole story. Despite offering preplanned and structured ways of achieving prescribed learning outcomes, many exercises can create problems for the unwary. The purpose of this section is to draw attention to some of these possible pitfalls and by doing so, offer you, through increased awareness, the opportunity to avoid these dangers.

Which reality?

One of the most problematic areas in the use of facilitative exercises arises from their preplanned and pre-structured character. The problem is that they can easily overlay the students' learning agenda with an agenda of their own. What may have felt relevant and important to the designer of the exercise may not be as relevant or important to the participant.

The exercise necessarily presumes learning outcomes and these are often stated as part of the exercise framework. Questions should be asked concerning how appropriate these anticipated learning outcomes are to the course at hand and the needs of the students on it.

Linked to this is the associated problem that exercises often have little similarity with real life and as such require links to be forged between the learning generated by the exercise and its application to real-world issues, problems and experiences. The more difficult it becomes to forge those links and the more tenuous those links appear to the student, the less credible the exercise will be as a vehicle for effective learning which is readily transferable to the real world of the student.

Opening a can of worms

Another danger, particularly with exercises which seek to encourage student disclosure, is that participation in the exercise can lead to students exposing quite deeply held feelings and experiences. Such disclosure requires skilled and sensitive feedback in a supportive environment. You should think long and hard about how easy it would be for you to provide this necessary support within the framework of the course you are planning.

Overexposure

On a long course which utilizes a series of facilitative and experiential exercises, there can be the possibility that students will suffer from exercise overexposure. They may simply get tired of moving from participation in one exercise and subsequent feedback, to involvement in another without the learning pattern being broken up by variations in facilitative method.

This problem can also arise from a facilitative approach based on the view that exercises are a 'total method'. By this we mean an approach where facilitative exercises are the only means adopted of encouraging student learning.

Too much to deal with

Exercises can generate an enormous amount of material and this itself can be a problem in that there is insufficient time to make the most of all the work created. This is particularly true of courses which have lots of participants as, obviously, with each participant responding to the elements of the exercise they are involved in, you will have as many sets of responses as you do participants. Feeding-back 20 sets of findings takes a great deal of time if each is to be done justice. In turn, dealing with some students' work and not others' creates its own problems.

Exercises which are structured to allow for group response may offer a simple solution for large group courses, as splitting a group of 20 into four groups results in only four sets of grouped responses, a far more manageable prospect for all concerned.

Familiar feedback

All too often, facilitators make great efforts to ensure that the exercises they use offer variety for learners but the same cannot be said of associated feedback. The problem comes when, after a stimulating activity, students are asked to return to a feedback phase which is exactly the same in structure to previous feedback sessions.

This familiar feedback is often in the form of a plenary discussion of the exercise, with the questions following a routinized pattern which seeks to unpack the exercise experience and encourage students to work their way around the experiential learning cycle. Alternatively, it involves (often necessarily) a review of students' work requiring the group to work their way through flipchart group work.

You will find that time spent thinking about improving the way exercises are fed back will often prove rewarding not only for your students but also for you as the facilitator.

If they're active they must be working

Another impression that exercises can foster is that, because of the high levels of activity they promote, facilitative exercises must be good at getting students working. This impression arises from the misconception that groups that are actively engaged on some learning task are working effectively.

This can mask a situation where activity arises from students simply responding to the requirements of the exercise; it cannot therefore be taken as an accurate measure of how much effective learning actually flows from the exercise itself.

We have both had experiences of running exercises which generate huge amounts of student activity but little in the way of effective student learning as a result. The question should therefore be not how much are the students being encouraged to do but how much of what they are being asked to do is worthwhile.

The long haul

There is a rule of thumb which says that, to be effective, an exercise needs to have a feedback phase twice as long as the exercise it is feeding back. Generally speaking we are not in favour of such hard-and-fast rules but this one does raise an important issue. Exercises are not ends in themselves but are means to an end, that end being to encourage effective student learning which is hopefully relevant, significant and meaningful to the participant.

But effective learning is often not possible within the immediate and unfolding nature of the exercise itself; instead it requires reflection and this reflection arises from carefully structured and managed feedback. Such feedback takes time, perhaps twice as long as the exercise, perhaps more but seldom less.

We have often found that what happens in reality is that facilitators get so wrapped up in the running of the exercise, particularly where that exercise seems to be going extremely well, that they allow the time spent doing the exercise to eat into the time they had allocated for feedback. This in turn results in superficial or rushed feedback (or both!) which, as a consequence, undermines the potential effective learning which may have resulted from a more balanced and more closely time-managed session.

The whole subject of feedback as it relates to exercises is covered in much greater detail in the next chapter.

Forced participation

Students attending a facilitative course are in many ways a captive audience and, by virtue of both explicit and implicit group rules and expectations, students often feel that their involvement as participants in facilitative exercises is a requirement they cannot avoid.

This feeling of being forced to participate can have unfortunate consequences on the level of real involvement and the resultant learning that takes place. Let's face it, students often feel more comfortable and safer as a face in a crowd of fellow participants, firmly planted in their seat. Exercises wrench them out of this comfort zone and force them to work with others and to contribute their own thoughts and feelings as part of a bigger group effort.

Problems arising from this feeling of forced participation are often best dealt with openly and honestly at the outset within a session designed to deal with this and associated issues of participation, commitment, involvement and honesty. The use of a developmental programme of exercises which eases students into more demanding and challenging exercise roles, can also assist.

Rigidity

It must be remembered that exercises already have their own internal structure, aim and associated time-frame based upon design assumptions about what is likely to happen when the exercise is run. These assumptions may be based on limited testing in the real world by the exercise designer and as such may not prove very accurate for you and your students.

For example, an exercise may throw up unforeseen learning which, while 'off-track' as far as the design is concerned, is both pertinent and valuable to the course content as far as both you and your students are concerned. Such instances can be problematic from the vantage point of flexibility. Do you jeopardize the exercise process by stopping off to address this valid and valuable issue, or do you risk losing the moment by pushing it onto the back burner to be addressed later, after the exercise is complete?

One way of resolving this is to give the decision to the group and shift responsibility for learning choices onto them. Another is to flag up the risks involved and explain the reasons for making the decision that you have.

Unrealistic strategies and solutions

A rarely considered difficulty with facilitative exercises is that while they encourage students to work through experiential forms of learning activity in the hope of leading them towards learning outcomes, developing solutions and strategies to problems along the way, rarely is much thought given as to how realistic these strategies and solutions are when applied in the real world. What must be remembered is that if learning is to be effective, it must stand the test of being transferred from the safe and controlled learning environment of the course room to the harsh and more challenging environment of the learner's real world.

What we would seek to encourage is the inclusion of an additional learning phase within which ideas, strategies, solutions and recipes for action are tested for useability and applicability in that real world. There is a need for questions such as, 'How realistic is this strategy?' or, 'How true is this conclusion of your own experiences outside this course?' as well as others such as, 'Just how easy will this solution or idea be to apply in the real world?' and, 'What might get in the way of applying this recipe for action in my workplace?'

OVERCOMING THE LIMITATIONS INHERENT IN EXERCISES

We have gone into some detail in considering the possible dangers and inherent shortcomings of facilitative exercises in an effort to encourage you to think carefully about how you come to choose and use such exercises in your own facilitative work. As we said at the beginning, an awareness of these dangers can go a long way to ensuring that you sidestep pitfalls and avoid problems before they arise. In addition to awareness, there are things you can do to ensure that the exercises you decide to utilize create and maximize lasting learning.

Relevance

Earlier in this chapter we mentioned that a key phase in learning for the student is the forging of links between their existing knowledge, skills and experiences and new information and new ways of thinking about and dealing with issues, ideas and problems. It follows therefore, that to get the most from their participation in exercises and the experiences that these provide, it is necessary for each student to see the relevance of what they are doing and to anticipate how such learning might be usefully applied to everyday issues and problems.

Thus the decision to employ a particular exercise ought to take this need for relevance into account. How difficult or easy will it be for students to make necessary links between the learning that arises and the real-world context within which it will find use through application? Does the planned exercise fit into the flow of learning at that point and complement the overall developmental process of learning taking place? Questions should also be asked concerning the relevance of the exercise to stated course aims and planned learning intentions.

Significance

Another important consideration concerns the significance of the learning that might follow from the use of the planned exercise for the participants concerned. By this we mean the extent to which the planned learning outcomes of the exercise serve to progress the student's learning by introducing new learning and increasing development.

Learning should be of consequence to the learner; it should make a difference, allowing him or her to move forward through personal progress and development in the area being addressed. As such, any planned use of specific exercises should also be reviewed in terms of their potential significance in the learning process.

Meaningfulness

To be useful and useable, exercises must also be meaningful for the participants in that they should makes sense and be understandable. There will be instances where the real consequences and main learning from an exercise will only come to be revealed during feedback, but facilitators should also think carefully about the effect on learner motivation of an exercise which makes little real sense at the time to the participants involved.

Meets learner's needs

The more flexible your course plan the more responsive your facilitation becomes and this in turn will enable you to insert appropriate exercises in places on the course indicated not by a course plan but by the learning needs of your students at that juncture. It is far more effective to direct learning in response to unfolding need than to try to steer students against the flow of their needs purely because you have an exercise planned. Often you will find that a key learning opportunity arises within a particular phase which needs exploring and would benefit from student-centred activity in the process; this is where a working knowledge of an array of facilitative activities and exercises coupled with a responsive course plan will stand you in good stead.

Encourage useful and useable contributions

They say the proof of the pudding is in the eating and this is true of facilitated learning. In this case the eating is actually the application of learning gained from the course to the problems existing in the everyday real worlds of the students. Your choice of exercise should reflect this requirement by encouraging learning and developing ideas, solutions and strategies which will be useful and useable to the student outside of the training setting.

Allow time for constructive and effective feedback

We won't pre-empt the next chapter which explores the issue of feedback in detail.

ICE-BREAKERS AND ENERGIZERS

Ice-breakers

The beginning of any facilitated training session is often a tense and awkward time for both student and facilitator alike, particularly where participants have not met before. This apprehension and anxiety must be dealt with before the group can begin to work together at an effective level, and this is where ice-breakers can be of real use, breaking down initial barriers to learning by introducing people to each other and getting them actively working together.

Ice-breaking exercises form an important part of the learning process. All too often they are relegated from the premier division to the minor leagues of facilitation as 'bolted-on' afterthoughts; they may even be missed altogether. The latter approach seems to be based on the assumption that adult learners can manage this phase on their own, naturally coming together to introduce themselves, find out about each others' backgrounds and so on. The truth is that this rarely happens. This can cause an acute problem where a course or seminar is short. It may be that you have only half a day, or one day, to achieve your planned learning intentions. In such circumstances you will need to get the ice broken quickly to enable the group to move forward in a more relaxed and effective way.

Don't ignore the possibility that apparently already formed groups won't have any ice to break. It is our experience that groups who seem to know each other already will often benefit from getting to know each other better. Another occasion when ice-breaking is necessary is where you, the facilitator, are coming into a group which is already formed: you will need to get to know the members, and they you, if a relationship of trust is to be formed.

This trust will be important for later learning and a significant factor in its development will be the breaking down of barriers to honesty and communication which might exist within the learning group at the outset. If carefully planned and managed, ice-breaking can also have the effect of challenging the stereotyping and labelling which can occur in the early phases of a course, the result of people's initial impressions of each other. Lengthy periods of student inactivity at the outset of the course when a course overview is provided, learning intentions are outlined and a group learning contract agreed, can mean that members of the group have little opportunity or inclination to say or do anything. An ice-breaking exercise can be just the thing to help them to start to come out of themselves. Of course the type of exercise you run will have a considerable effect on this and later participation and learning.

You need to ensure that any ice-breaker exercises you run are relevant to the group. If they also have some direct relevance to the purpose of the course then so much the better, and this will be made considerably easier if you have planned carefully and found out as much as you can about the learning group beforehand.

For some students, ice-breaking exercises can be significant learning events in themselves. People who are naturally shy and feel in some way inadequate or overawed by other members of the group, can gain early confidence from learning that they can, in fact, talk to strangers quite freely and that the experience is not nearly as daunting as they might at first have imagined. Learners might also be unused to working closely with other people and may find an early and safe introduction to team-building very useful.

Apart from the particular objective of breaking the ice, these exercises should generally be straightforward and, although not shrinking from raising important issues, should generally aim to provide a facility for members to meet and speak with each other in an informal and safe activity, while at the same time introducing aspects of course content. A good rule of thumb to measure whether your ice-breaker is pitched at the right level is whether or not there is a need to feed it back (process it or unpack it); if you do, then the activity is probably pitched too high. An exception to this rule is when you are training trainers. While they are, in one sense, involved in the content, they also need to be able to take a step back and view the exercise for its educational implications.

Some hints on using ice-breakers

- Realize their place in the learning process and their importance in breaking down barriers to learning, group cohesion and communication.
- Keep them active. Ice-breakers can often meet the need for people to introduce themselves, learn about each others' backgrounds and become familiar with names.
- Get the group to brainstorm what they would like to know about each other (keep this at a fairly basic and relevant level) and then make this the basis for a getting-to-know-you session.
- Make ice-breakers work for you by including appropriate issues but at an introductory level.
- Keep them straightforward and explain their use to the group.
- Remember a rule-of-thumb: if you need to feedback your ice-breaking activities they are probably pitched too high (unless you are training trainers).

Energizers

Even when you have been doing something interesting and enjoyable, like reading a good book, after a while your concentration and enthusiasm begin to tail off. This is often an indication that you need to take a break or have a change of activity – maybe make a cup of coffee or walk the dog. This is also true of energy levels in your learning group which, from time to time, may need a boost. This is where energizers come in, activities which offer a change of momentum or direction.

Group energizers can take many forms and you should keep an open mind about which activities might be suitable. They should offer

- a high degree of student involvement
- one or more changes of activity
- the opportunity for students to move around rather than just sitting and talking
- the opportunity to re-focus the group's attention back on the issues at hand.

A good example would be a quick-fire brainstorm on a new but related subject, run in such a way that students left their seats and recorded their own ideas on flip-chart paper or 'newsprint' attached to the wall.

An important aspect of skilful facilitation is the ability to keep in touch with the mood and energy of the group, monitoring its momentum by gauging non-verbal messages, levels of involvement and commitment to the work in hand, by staying attuned to signs that concentration and enthusiasm may be dropping.

As we said above, the ice-breaker(s) you choose should have the effect of stimulating the group into working energetically. After this point it is perfectly normal for the energy level of the group to rise and fall, and this can be due to a number of factors. We have found that it is not unusual for the level to fall after a long feedback session following an exercise. Typically the students will have been working well; disclosure and lots of supportive group interaction will have been taking place. It would not be unusual for the group to become increasingly reflective until either the facilitator or group member will suggest that a break is taken and the 'spell' will be broken. After such a break the group may need to be refocused with an energizing exercise.

Other typical times for energy levels to flag are after lunch and towards the end of the day. After lunch, a longer energizing activity may be indicated. At the end of the day you may, if it is within your discretion, need to be flexible about the finish time. Failing this you will need to keep energy high enough for the learning to be meaningful. Be aware of the needs of learners in their real world. Your course members may have a bus or train to catch, they may need to pop into the supermarket on their way home or today might be their birthday. Whatever the reason, remember that your students, like you, have a life outside the group and it plays an increasingly important role in their thinking as the day gets nearer to its end.

Some hints on using energizers

- Keep in touch with the energy levels of your learning group. Watch out for the tell-tale signs of flagging attention, reduced participation and/or enthusiasm.
- Be aware of, and plan for, the times when group energy is particularly low, after lunch for example, at the close of the day or towards the end of the course.
- Energizers, by their very nature, should be lively, active sessions which provide an opportunity to refocus and change the pace.
- Avoid the use of games or activities that make students feel overly self-conscious or silly.
- Try not to confuse discomfort within the group when confronting difficult issues with falling energy levels. Signs of withdrawal or lack of enthusiasm may suggest that students are trying to avoid challenging aspects of the course.

CORE EXERCISES

In closing we would like to turn to a form of exercise that we call the 'core exercise'. The idea behind core exercises forms part of an exciting new type of facilitation that we have developed, appropriately named 'Real World Facilitation'. This new approach of encouraging learning is fully explained in our first book entitled *A Practical Guide to Facilitation Skills: A Real World Approach* (1993, published by Kogan Page).

Core exercises are characterized by the fact that they offer a more flexible exercise framework than conventional forms of exercise, providing a core structure to which students can bring their own ideas, issues, experiences and problems. Such exercises encourage students to use these aspects of their own personal learning agenda as the very material with which to undertake the exercise itself. Accordingly, the core exercise supports relevant, significant and meaningful learning by ensuring that the exercise is nothing more than an effective learning vehicle which the student uses to work through his or her own learning needs.

An example of this approach would be where the facilitator has preplanned a role-play exercise, but has left the actual details of the scenario to be generated by the learners. Alternatively, the facilitator may decide to move into a learning phase where students move into small groups to discuss an issue that has arisen. Although it is the facilitator who has decided in which way the learning process will proceed, ideally the content of that unplanned discussion will have been suggested by contributions made by members of the group.

Not all of the exercises in this volume are core exercises but many are. What we would encourage you to do is to consider the exercises you already use in the light of our description of a core exercise, and decide how much space each allows for the working through of the students' own pressing and immediate learning needs in the area being addressed. If the exercise forces the student to work through a fixed and pre-set learning process which has clearly defined learning outcomes and requires links to the real world to be forged by facilitator and student, chances are such exercises are the reverse of what core exercises should be.

CHAPTER 3

How to feed the exercises back

INTRODUCTION

You will hear time and again that facilitated exercises are only as good as the feedback that comes after them. We cannot stress too strongly that with all the planning in the world, the most intricately designed and exquisitely executed exercises are nothing without feedback.

We have witnessed full-scale exercises which would have done NATO proud, but after several hours of activity there was a cursory, 'Well, what did we get out of that?'– and it was all over.

Feedback is facilitation in its purest sense. It is the act of transposing experience into meaningful learning. It is what you as facilitator will be expected by your learners to be skilled in; it is where you earn your money.

After you have finished reading this chapter we hope you will feel confident about feedback in terms of:

- Helping learners with the process of describing what happened in the exercise.
- Encouraging reflection with a view to making sense of the experience.
- Focusing on the consequences of the learning for the learner and assisting in forming strategies to use it.

ASSISTING THE LEARNER WITH THE PROCESS OF DESCRIBING WHAT HAPPENED IN THE EXERCISE

One very important aspect of feedback is the initial phase of agreeing with the group members what actually took place. Unless there is agreement on what actually happened, you cannot hope to get the most learning from it. It is also useful to identify if there are any differing perceptions of what happened in the exercise. So you need to invest a little time in doing this properly.

Here is just one suggested system that you can follow, although you will probably want to adapt it to suit your own situation, needs and ability.

- Start by reviewing the aim and objectives of the exercise. You outline for the participants what it was intended to cover and take them through it stage by stage. A good prompt we have found is to make use of the method instructions which you will find with each of the exercises in this binder.
- Move on to getting individuals within the group to describe what happened as they saw it. It is important at this stage that no one tries to interpret what happened, especially you the facilitator. The whole point of this stage of the process is to establish the facts of what happened and which all the group agree to. Interpretation now will just get in the way of subsequent understanding. Concentrate on any physical activity which took place, what was said, what was achieved and note any particular non-verbal behaviour that was spotted (but don't interpret).
- Identify any differences in perceptions and seek consensus from the group about what happened and what was said. If any issues emerge which seem to be key issues to the purpose of the exercise, then it would be a good idea to record these on a flipchart so that everyone can see what was said or what was raised.

Note: if the exercise you are running is fairly lengthy, it is quite likely that some of the detail will be missed at this stage. As a precaution, it is a good idea for you to make notes as the exercise progresses and use them to refer to later and help jog memories.

ENCOURAGING REFLECTION WITH A VIEW TO MAKING SENSE OF THE EXPERIENCE

After investing time in establishing what happened in the exercise, what was said and what issues were raised, the next stage of the feedback loop is to spend time encouraging reflection and helping the participants make real sense of what happened with a view to extracting as much learning as possible from it.

This stage of the loop is both vital and potentially lengthy, and there are a number of issues which could get in the way of it being effective. So in the discussion which follows we will go into this aspect of feedback in more detail.

You the facilitator are aiming to encourage the participants or learners in your group to *disclose*. This means that they are being encouraged to talk about the experience they have undergone and in doing so disclose to the group whatever feelings they may have had about the experience, any attitudes it may have revealed to themselves or others, or any links with their personal experience that may have been made. In this last respect participants may confirm what they knew already, or have some of their cherished views challenged. This type of learning can be painful, emotional, cathartic or gentle – it all depends, but what is certain is that you the facilitator will need to guide, support and encourage the learner through the process.

Disclosure involves individuals unearthing their own experiences, revealing their opinions and attitudes and describing their behaviour. Then, often with the help of the group and guided by the facilitator, the students are encouraged to make sense of their experiences, reflect on the validity and appropriateness of their disclosed attitudes and to understand the consequences of their behaviour, turning this into valuable and useable learning.

Here are some hints on facilitating student disclosure:

- Concentrate on encouraging the disclosure of real-world problems, issues and experiences which bear directly on the subject of the training being undertaken. For example, if you are running a training course which is focusing on management issues and skills, then establish what relevant experience and skills your participants already hold in this field.
- Select exercises which will maximize the learner's opportunities to raise and explore their own real-world problems, issues and experiences.
- Use your facilitation to place disclosure into the learners' context. One way of achieving this is to consciously ask the learners for examples from their own experience, of what they mean. Many of the feedback questions we have provided with the exercises will help you do this. These are generally specific to the exercises in question. We offer below some transferable ideas, however, which you might find useful.

Disclosing feelings

- How does the person feel about holding this view?
- How does she or he think others might feel, knowing she or he felt that way?
- What was she or he feeling when ... happened?
- Can the person recall what she or he felt when ... was said?

Note of caution: we do not subscribe to the school of facilitation which looks for participants to reveal their feelings in everything. Perpetually asking a learner what they feel becomes intrusive, meaningless and frankly boring. It has in our view partly been responsible for giving facilitation in some quarters the undeserved reputation of being unnecessarily 'touchy feely', and psychotherapeutic. Bear in mind the need to respect a person's right not to say how they are feeling about a particular issue.

Identify real-world consequences

Disclosure can further be encouraged by exploring:

- What are the implications of what happened, or what was said in the participants' role?
- How compatible is this view with the values and purpose of the person's organization?
- How will the person work with someone who expresses an opposite view?

Sensitively challenge the participants

- Question the validity of the views expressed.
- On what is the view based?
- How would the person challenge this view for him or herself or in another?
- What are the consequences of holding such a view?

Help the participants reflect on the process of change

- Does the person or group doing the reflecting want to change?

(Remember that being a reflective practitioner is all about change.)

- What are the barriers to change? Are they people, attitudes, structures, ... what?
- What might assist change?
- Who will support change?
- Are strategies for change achievable, realistic and workable?

A sure sign of a positive, energetic group is one which is starting to discuss and disclose and getting to grips with some of the issues outlined above. This is at the core of feedback. One reason you are reading this is presumably that you find facilitation to be a useful learning medium in that unlike other media, students on a facilitated course have an opportunity to vocalize their feelings, thoughts and attitudes in a way that enables and encourages reflective learning.

Drawing on learners' experiences as examples

We noted above the importance of drawing on the learner's own examples from experience and anchoring the learning in the real world.

By asking for a real-world example, you the facilitator can draw upon the learner's own experiences to both clarify an important issue and to place this within the context of a live training session where its meaning and relevance can be explored.

There are several potential obstacles to good quality disclosure and therefore learning. Two of these obstacles need a little more analysis and advice on how to overcome them. We have called them 'the comfort zone' and 'avoidance'.

The comfort zone

None of us likes feeling uncomfortable, especially in a group of people, some of whom we know and perhaps work with on a day-to-day basis. Normally, people feel safe in the knowledge that their views, opinions and beliefs will remain unchallenged, hidden from view or simply taken at face value. Although they may underpin our ways of thinking about and behaving towards others, our beliefs, opinions and attitudes seldom become the focus of our own or others' attention. We generally feel comfortable in the knowledge that, by-and-large, people will take us as they find us.

This is not the case within the learning environment, particularly on courses which deal with issues such as interpersonal behaviour and relationships, or those that consider equal opportunities and fair treatment. Likewise, training in assertiveness, management, team-building and many other similar subjects are bound to include exercises and learning activities which are designed to encourage personal reflection and disclosure of students' views, thoughts and feelings on important and often contentious issues. Many of the exercises in this binder will raise such issues.

Feelings of safety and security can and do evaporate as learners are encouraged to step outside the familiarity of everyday relationships into the stark and revealing area beyond this comfort zone. This is the reality of being a participant on a facilitated training course which aims to encourage learners to disclose, consider and then begin to address real and pressing issues.

When students are asked to reflect on their own views, feelings and past behaviour in this way and to discuss these issues with the learning group, various thoughts and concerns about the topic under discussion can emphasize vulnerability and heighten anxiety for some learners.

Why do people prefer to stay in the comfort zone? Here are a few reasons:

- Fear of having one's views attacked or questioned.
- Lack of conformity with accepted or encouraged values ('I don't agree, but I don't want to be out on a limb').
- Lack of commitment ('It's not an issue/big enough issue ... I don't feel strongly ... I can't get worked up about it').
- Feeling of risk-taking ('Too much of a risk ... I'm not ready').
- Fear of being misunderstood despite support for accepted or encouraged values ('I can't express what I want to say and it might come out all wrong').
- Fear of alignment with unpopular 'standard bearers' ('I don't want to be associated with them even though I agree with their position').
- Lack of knowledge ('I should know').
- Lack of skill and its associated embarrassment ('I feel I should be able to do this').

- Embarrassment at disclosure ('I don't feel comfortable telling others/showing others what I think or feel').
- Too hard ('This is too much like hard work; I prefer an easy life/way out/option').

These are just a few of the reasons why learners might want to remain protected by the force-field of their comfort zone. You may not always hear the reasons expressed in quite the same way as in the examples we have given above. There are many other different ways in which students will indicate to you that they wish to remain comfortable and safe; a few are listed below as illustrations:

- Outright refusal to take part, eg: 'I simply don't want to discuss gay rights!' or, 'I am not getting involved in that exercise, it's silly'.
- Apparent reluctance to take part, displayed either verbally, or more likely non-verbally, eg: averting eye-contact with facilitator, or adopting a closed body position.
- Questioning the validity of the exercise or topic being discussed.
- Questioning the need for the exercise or the need to cover that topic, eg: 'Is it necessary to talk about empathy; can't we get on?'
- Questioning detail (as illustrated above).
- Involvement, but at a safer, less disclosive or risky level.
- Flight, ie: laughing off a serious issue, making a joke rather than giving an honest and open response.
- Asking a question of the facilitator rather than answering one. (Note though, that a genuine question seeking clarification or knowledge would not display an attempt to remain in the comfort zone.)

One or more of these indicators may be present where a learner is trying to stay comfortable. Having recognized that it is happening it will be for you to work out a strategy to help the learner through it. Because the way of dealing with learners who want to stay comfortable is so similar to dealing with the other problem, avoidance, we will look at avoidance first and then briefly consider the strategies you might adopt to deal with both.

Avoidance

The second obstacle to effective disclosure as part of the feedback loop is avoidance. Staying-put in the safe, known and familiar comfort zone, is certainly one means by which students avoid having to confront and deal with real and significant issues and problems which impact upon the real world of everyday life. In many ways the comfort zone can be likened to a force-field, shielding the student from exposure to new and challenging ways of both looking at and dealing with existing issues and problems. In this sense, strategies of avoidance serve as the vehicle by which students seek either to remain within, or return behind the force-field of safety.

Below is a summary of strategies of avoidance that facilitators can experience within the training setting:

- Obvious silence – where one or more, or perhaps all of the group engage in deliberate silence; in extreme cases even in response to direct questions.
- Tone of voice – aggressive, hesitant, cynical, dismissive or jocular.
- Gestures – both facial and body gestures.
- Non-verbal indications of avoidance may include lack of eye-contact, looking away (particularly down at the floor), shifting about on the seat, hiding the mouth with a hand, pretending to read a document with great interest, tapping and fidgeting, sitting back with arms (and maybe legs) crossed.
- 'We' statements, where the person seeks to speak on behalf of others and in so doing avoids taking responsibility for their own views and attitudes.
- Scapegoating/transference by transferring blame onto the victim or other object which might on examination prove inappropriate or invalid.
- False concern for process – trying to steer the course away from an area which is uncomfortable or challenging
- Identifying with others – persistent agreement or identification with the thoughts of others.
- Ridiculing the contributions of other participants.

Note. It is always worth remembering that subtle non-verbal behaviour is easy to misunderstand; it should only be used as a guide and needs supporting indicators. It can be a mistake to assume that actions necessarily speak louder than words. Also, cultural differences can frustrate accurate interpretation of the meaning of gestures and other non-verbal messages.

Facilitator avoidance

Don't forget that you the facilitator can also adopt strategies to ensure that the course or the feedback don't stray into 'difficult' waters. A number of facilitator avoidance strategies can be identified; these include:

- Focusing on members of the group felt to be 'safe' by the facilitator, ie: those who won't ask difficult questions, or make contentious contributions.
- An unnecessarily rigid adherence to the stated course aim and planned learning outcomes as a means of cutting off particular avenues of discussion.
- Arguing that something isn't important when the truth is that it is too challenging.
- A deliberate refocusing of the group through a change of activity when it becomes clear that the outcome of the current exercise will be difficult to facilitate.
- A move away from activity-based learning for the student to more didactic input such as mini lectures or showing a video for the purpose of re-establishing control.
- Not following up on contributions that might lead towards issues the facilitator would rather avoid.
- Ignoring the non-verbal signals from group members which clearly suggest avoidance.

How to deal with avoidance and encourage people to move out of the comfort zone

Strategies of avoidance, if left unchecked, create significant barriers to effective learning. We suggest a five-point plan for dealing with avoidance which is sufficiently flexible to account for and address many of the avoidance strategies described here and others you may have experience of, or have studied. It is given in summary here but is fully developed in *A Practical Guide to Facilitation Skills* (Spinks and Clements, 1993, published by Kogan Page).

- Noticing
- Interpreting
- Addressing

- Allowing feedback
- Encouraging involvement, disclosure or risk-taking.

You will see that it is really a feedback loop within a loop.

Noticing

The most fundamental step in coping with avoidance is being aware of it. Keep in touch with both spoken and unspoken messages and the nature of interactions between learners.

Interpreting

Take care to think through exactly why you have formed the impression that a participant is showing signs of avoidance. What are the messages you have picked up on? Is there a possibility that you have wrongly interpreted them? Are there alternative reasons for the behaviour (tiredness or overload for example)? Remember that saying something like, 'I see you are angry' is not the same as, 'I notice you reacted quite strongly to that last comment; are you angry?'

Addressing

If avoidance becomes apparent as the course develops, you can address the issue with the group in a non-specific way (ie, not identifying individuals or describing specific behaviour). This could be done by explaining aspects and examples of avoidance and its implications to the group in broad terms, while at the same time encouraging people to participate at the most honest, open and effective level by stressing the importance of student contributions to the learning process.

At times it may be necessary to address instances of avoidance directly with individual students in order that their behaviour can be explained to them directly. If this is done carefully, the very process of raising the learner's awareness of how their behaviour is perceived by others may be enough to overcome the barrier and encourage more open involvement.

Allowing feedback

Learners often need space to respond when their avoidance is reflected back to them by the facilitator or other members of the learning group. This reaction may be defensive, whereby such students try to justify their resistance to involvement or attempt to explain the behaviour away. Alternatively, they may clarify their behaviour and show that it did not amount to avoidance and has been wrongly interpreted.

Encouraging involvement, disclosure or risk-taking

However the student responds, it offers the facilitator a good and appropriate opportunity to reinforce the fundamental importance of individual involvement and its relationship to subsequent learning. If students want training that meets their needs, which is transferable to and useful within real-world situations, much flesh on the bones of the content which is to be addressed on the course must come from the students themselves. How else can it be ensured that the topics and issues discussed are directly relevant, significant and meaningful to the course members undertaking the training?

FOCUSING ON THE CONSEQUENCES OF THE LEARNING FOR THE LEARNER AND ASSISTING IN FORMING STRATEGIES TO USE IT

This is the last stage of the feedback loop, when the focus moves from learners describing what has happened and establishing what it means, to working through what they are going to do about it.

It has now become necessary to take students *beyond* this disclosive stage towards the point at which they begin to confront and address identified issues and problems, reflecting on the validity and real-world consequences of their attitudes and behaviour before finally working on realistic and workable strategies for dealing with them *where it counts*, in the real-world of everyday life beyond the learning group.

Do not leave the identification of real-world issues, problems and experiences too late; they should provide the very elements which your group will be working with during the course. You can think of it in terms of a real-world PIE, the ingredients of which are real world *Problems, Issues* and *Experiences*. At each stage get the real issues out, identify the real problems and *always* get the learners to share real examples of how this affects them in their everyday lives. This process of identification leads us into an area of facilitation which is fundamental to experiential learning: disclosure.

Opportunities should be taken wherever possible to illustrate and contextualize learner issues and to set possible strategies and solutions against such real-world examples, tasking students to reflect on whether they are workable, realistic and achievable in such circumstances *from the learner's point of view*.

In summary, you need to encourage learners to do the following.

1. *Clarify the nature of the issue or problem being focused upon.*

One of your roles is to make sure that there is no confusion in the mind of anybody in the group about the nature of the problems and challenges they are addressing. Identifying the nature of the problem being addressed is not always easy; there may be a number of alternatives. Some of the possibilities you will need to consider include:

- Is this a training problem?
- Is this a problem of attitude, for either the learner or the people with whom the learner will come into contact?
- Is this a problem associated with the structure of the organization; is something missing or is something going wrong?

There are of course many other possibilities, but suffice to say that if the true nature of the problem or challenge is correctly identified, then it will be considerably easier to work out an appropriate coping strategy with the learner.

2. *Identify how and when such issues and problems can and do arise and what can happen when they do.*

In this part of the process you will want to try and identify the times and reasons for the problems or issues to arise. This continues with the process of trying to find out as much as possible with a view to making an appropriate response.

For example, if the learner's problem is lack of ability to confront people with difficult information or feedback we would want to find out if this is always the case, or if are there any times when it is easier, such as when there is support available. Is the difficulty restricted to dealing with certain personality types or is it with all people, and so on.

3. *Guide the student into thinking about and formulating strategies and solutions to these identified issues and problems, which are achievable and realistic in a real-world setting.*

Here there is a word of caution to be said at the outset. It is all too easy for learners on courses which have been facilitated to become idealistic about what can be achieved. We have experienced this many times in the context of equal opportunities training, where learners may for the first time have had a significant experience in discovering the real meaning of various types of unfairness. It is not uncommon for this to lead to them wanting to go back to their organization with a kind of missionary zeal which will fall flat as surely as leaving the lid off a lemonade bottle.

Keep the learners anchored in the real world. Strategies for change need to take in to account:

- the skill level and commitment of the learners
- their strength of character
- the nature, ethos and values of the organization they are in.

Help them to keep objectives straightforward and most of all achievable; in this way they will become much longer-lasting and fulfilled agents for change than if they go back to attempt the impossible and just burn out.

Part II

Activities

1. AGREEING THE ISSUES

Time guide: 45 minutes

Participants: 15–20

Equipment and resources:
Pen and paper for each student; 'Agreeing the Issues' worksheet

Application:
Equal opportunities training
Staff development training
Management training
Interpersonal skills training
Assertiveness training
Quality of service training

Category:
Encouraging learning through openness (attitudes, feelings)

Aim

The exercise aims to encourage students to work through an issues clarification and agenda setting process whereby, through their responses to the questions provided in the worksheet, they identify the issues most immediate, pressing and relevant to them.

Issues raised by this exercise

By its very nature this is an issues clarification exercise and, as such, the issues raised will depend on the responses students give to the questions provided.

Method

You should start by explaining the aim to your students and issuing the worksheet to each, allowing them to clarify any aspect of it they don't understand or have difficulty with.

Brief the students by explaining that this is a pairs exercise in which members of each pair will take it in turns to ask the other the questions on the worksheet, recording their responses for future reference. Each student can have 15 minutes to answer.

When both students have answered all the questions on the worksheet the group should break while you collate the key responses on a flipchart or whiteboard.

After the break the group should reform and there should then be a facilitated discussion of the findings with a view to setting a form of learning agenda from the issues raised. The important task is to clarify which of the issues identified are of most pressing importance to the group as a whole and thus deserve time being spent on them.

You may feel that it is important to either insert your own issues or to exert some control over the weighting process so as to ensure, by either of these interventions, that all the important areas get covered regardless of how challenging they might be.

Variations

You may wish to vary the group structure, changing from pairs to small groups depending on the size of the larger group.

Feedback advice

Feedback should be in the form of summarizing agreement and plotting some sort of path through the agenda constructed.

WORKSHEET

Agreeing the issues

What do you want to know about this subject?

What do you need to know about this subject?

Have you done any training in this area before; if so what?

What issues have most relevance for you personally?

What issues have most relevance for you professionally?

If you had to choose three of the most important aspects of this subject, which three would you choose?

Which issues cause problems for you in your everyday life?

Do you have experience of dealing with issues in this area; if so what are they?

2. Anonymous disclosure

Time guide: 45 minutes–1 hour

Participants: 15–20

Equipment and resources:
'Anonymous Disclosure' examples sheet. Students will also need a pen and paper to record their reactions to the statements.

Application:
Equal opportunities training
Staff development training
Management training
Interpersonal skills training
Assertiveness training
Quality of service training

Category:
Encouraging learning through openness (attitudes, feelings)

Aim

To identify honest reactions and responses to potentially challenging or controversial topics through anonymous disclosure. Also to provide the group with an indication of the range of views held within the group on a given topic and, through such consideration, to increase their awareness of both their own views and the views of others while also exploring the possible consequences of the views identified.

Issues raised by this exercise

Self and group disclosure.

Method

Explain the aim of the exercise to the group and emphasize the anonymous nature of the disclosure sought. Ask students to only record reactions which are *honest* and *immediate*.
Ensure that each student has pen and paper to record their reactions to statements. Explain that no personal details should be entered.

Read out the statement you have chosen which may either be one provided on the 'Anonymous Disclosure' examples sheet or one of your own design. Encourage each student to record an immediate, honest reaction to what has been said on the reaction sheet, then collect each sheet in.

Give the group a short break (perhaps a coffee break if this is appropriate). During the break you should prepare a flipchart which shows the range of reactions obtained in response to the statement read out.

Gather the group together and run a plenary discussion on the findings. We suggest that students be encouraged to discuss not only the findings but also the potential consequences of particular views expressed through the exercise. Attention could also be drawn to the question of changing attitudes and the permanence of such change.

Variations

Rather than feedback in plenary sessions, the group could be split up and tasked to discuss certain findings which they are assigned or choose to deal with.

Feedback advice

The anonymous nature of the exercise should allow students to feel safer in their level of disclosure. It is important during feedback not to threaten this by seeking individuals to own their reactions. Agree with the group that the reactions provided by individuals are a group learning resource and material with which to work.

EXAMPLES SHEET

Anonymous disclosure

Important note: These statements are designed to encourage student response so they are necessarily extreme or provocative. They should only be used as a learning resource in circumstances which encourage such views to be challenged.

'Women are less ambitious than men, generally speaking.'

'Black people are more lazy than white people.'

'Stuff about listening to other people and being sensitive about their feelings is just touchy-feely nonsense.'

'Equal opportunities has gone too far, minorities are getting all the chances and opportunities.'

'Homosexuality is a sickness and gay men and lesbians are sick.'

'Staff need to be chased up; people will only work hard if they think the manager is watching them.'

'Immigrants come over here and steal all our jobs.'

'I can hold what attitudes I want as long as I don't let them affect my behaviour.'

'Sometimes you have to be economical with the truth.'

'The only way to motivate people to do their best is through money.'

'The customer is always right.'

'Women should not get promoted as they don't stay that long, leaving either to get married or to have kids.'

'Women should stop at home looking after the kids and the house and leave the breadwinning to their menfolk.'

'The management have no idea what goes on, they're too detached from day-to-day issues and problems.'

3. ARE YOU BEING SERVED?

Time guide: 45 minutes

Participants: Group of 5 or more

Equipment and resources:
Resource sheet given with this exercise
Pen and paper for students to record their findings

Application:
Equal opportunities training
Interpersonal skills training
Management training
Staff development training
Quality of service training

Category:
Encouraging learning through openness (attitudes, feelings)
Course closure

Aim

To identify from the point of view of a receiver of a service how it is to have a service delivered by someone who harbours prejudice against you as opposed to one who doesn't.

Issues raised by this exercise

Prejudice, discrimination, stereotyping, labelling and links between attitudes and values.

Method

This exercise is sometimes best done either side of a break such as a morning or afternoon coffee break. You need to feel confident to handle this one as it can produce emotive results. It does, however, put over a powerful message.

Phase 1

You must start by stressing that it is not the intention to use this exercise to identify the views of an individual but to draw some general conclusions from the group.

Issue the resource sheet to each participant. Brief them that they will be asked to be really honest and respond to a word image that will be created for them. They are to write down what comes into their heads when the image is given.

Give one or more of the following images:

In your mind's eye:

- You can see group of young black men apparently hanging around on a street corner.
- You can see two young men cuddling and kissing on a park bench.
- You can see a group of gypsy travellers driving up your road and starting to park on some waste land near your house.

Responses should be spontaneous and immediate. Accordingly, this phase should take us no more than five minutes. After they have done this, collect all the sheets in and ask the group to take a break.

Look through the sheets and for each of the images make a list of what has been written, with the most strongly positive reaction at the top working down to the most strongly negative at the bottom. This is probably best done on a flipchart or on the board.

Phase 2

When the learners return, ask them to reflect on the list(s) in turn.

You then challenge them to consider the following:

> If you were (are) a member of one of the minority groups we have been thinking about ... who would you prefer to be served by?

To assist learners, you may want to give each response a letter or number with which they may identify during the session.

Variations

If you can get hold of pictures which have strong images of minority groups, these can be more powerful than word descriptions.

There are many possible applications of the messages to be learned from this exercise. Make it real-world as far as possible by linking to the experience of your learners. You might change the question to:

'... who would you rather be treated by?' (Healthcare)
'... who would you rather be reported by?' (Policing)

'... who would you rather be interviewed by?' (Local Government Services)

Feedback advice

This exercise deals with the issue of attitudes and behaviour and the links between them. There is a point of view which many hold that they can maintain prejudiced attitudes, but that they do not let such attitudes affect their behaviour. Even if this were true (and the authors do not agree that it is) there is a case for saying that if we are to make our service delivery as fair and acceptable as we can then it is better *not* to put ourselves in the position of having to 'bolt down' our attitudes but to confront and deal with them at source.

Questions which will help to bring out the issues include:

'Is there a link between attitudes and behaviour?'
'If yes ... why; if no ... why not?'
'How strongly does what a person really think come across in their non-verbal behaviour?'
'Is this stronger or weaker than the verbal message?'

PARTICIPANTS' REACTION SHEET

Are you being served?

Write down your reaction to the image given.
Do not identify yourself in any way.

Write down your reaction to the image given.
Do not identify yourself in any way.

Write down your reaction to the image given.
Do not identify yourself in any way.

4. Attitude ballot

Time guide: 45 minutes

Participants: 15–20 maximum

Equipment and resources:
Four 'ballot' type boxes or trays with labels supplied in resource page(s). 'Issue cards' supplied in resource pages

Application:
Equal opportunities training

Category:
Encouraging learning through openness (attitudes, feelings)

Aim

To encourage students to reveal their views and opinions on important issues in a safe and non-threatening way.

Method

Phase 1

The aim of the exercise is explained to the group by the facilitator who should also outline the phases briefly.

Each group member should then be given one set of 'Issue cards' (cut from the sheets provided). Students should be told to carefully read through each 'Issue card', considering their response to it. It should be emphasized that they should stick with their first reaction as far as possible. Cards should then be put into the appropriate ballot boxes, with the student recording which card went where for later reference.

Phase 2

Results should be worked out and entered on a flipchart showing the range of responses to each issue.

Phase 3

Group members should then be given a chance to disclose their reactions to the issues and the reasons for their choices. Honesty and avoidance should also be raised if appropriate.

Phase 4

Either in full group or in small groups (pairs perhaps) students should then be encouraged to discuss with each other their different viewpoints on the issues and the possible consequences of holding certain attitudes. It will be particularly useful to encourage people with opposite views on an issue to speak together.

Feedback advice

As with most exercises, feedback phases often promote the most learning as it is here that students begin the process of looking back on the exercise and considering its consequences and relevances. Accordingly, plenty of time should be allocated to such phases. Attention should be paid to the possible consequences for students of holding certain views.

LABELS

Attitude ballot

I agree

I disagree

I strongly agree

I neither agree nor disagree

I strongly disagree

ISSUE CARDS

Attitude ballot

When in Rome do as the Romans do

This equal opportunities thing has gone too far the other way

Women disqualify themselves from taking up senior positions because they choose to interrupt their careers to start a family

Black people are far too sensitive about racism

The best way to get a good job these days is to be a black lesbian wheelchair user

There are many jobs that women simply can't do

Racism is much less of a problem these days

There's no harm in telling the odd racist joke; black and Asian people should lighten up

I don't think schools should acknowledge this guru and that guru's birthday; this is not India

If black and Asian people integrated more in our culture there would be less racism

They're putting ramps into our building so that disabled people can get in; what a waste of money

It's not fair that women should compete for promotion with me, they're second earners while I'm the only breadwinner in my family

ISSUE CARDS

Attitude ballot

It's well known that deaf people cannot speak, that's the condition isn't it, deaf and dumb	Black people are notoriously lazier than white people; this is because they come from a hot country when you have to take things slower	Women are the homemakers and men are the hunters
Women cannot expect to work full-time when they have children to collect from school and tea to make	When people come to this country they should adopt our way of dressing and eating, wearing all these saris and eating curry is not British	People who have a disability are to be pitied
My attitudes don't affect my behaviour	There are 3 million unemployed and living on the dole; I think we should send the immigrants back home, there's not enough jobs to go round	Our culture is being threatened by all these foreigners
I get paid for what I do, not what I think	Whenever I see a group of black young men walking down the street I keep a hand on my wallet	We should show more tolerance towards gay people

ISSUE CARDS

Attitude ballot

We are now a multi-cultural society and should be proud of that

It doesn't matter what gender your manager is, what matters is how good a manager they are

Being careful with your langguge is an important part of being fair and extending equal opportunities

The thing that disables those with disability most is the built environment

I could never have a woman as a boss

Our culture is becoming richer because of Afro-Caribbean and Asian influences

Positive discrimination is against the law

Gay men and lesbians deserve equal opportunities and fair treatment

Gypsies are entitled to equal opportunities

Putting up a girlie calendar on the office wall is insensitive

What's the age of consent for gay men got to do with equal opportunities?

Mixed-race marriages are wrong

5. Behaviour arrays

Time guide: 45 minutes–1 hour

Participants: 15–20

Equipment and resources: Nil

Application:
Equal opportunities training
Staff development training
Management training
Interpersonal skills training
Assertiveness training
Quality of service training

Category: Role play

Aim

To encourage learners to try out various levels of behaviour in a safe and non-threatening environment in order to cope effectively with problematic situations identified by them.

Issues raised by this exercise

This exercise is particularly useful for interpersonal and assertiveness work.

Method

You should explain the broad aim of the exercise and emphasize that the main idea is to practise and try out new ways of behaving in challenging situations. You should also take time to ensure that the group understands the need for support for those students actually participating.

The introductory phase that follows is optional. You may find that the need to use this exercise will arise spontaneously while you are facilitating other work with your students. For example, a student may, in the course of a discussion, disclose a situation in which he or she often feels unable to cope effectively or assert themselves, or alternatively they may feel that their reaction to a given incident is excessive and lacks control. In such circumstances, the need to explore this disclosure might provide the ideal opportunity to utilize this exercise.

Of key importance is the opportunity for an individual to test out various levels of behaviour and response within the same scenario to see how they affect the role player's response. To enable this to happen, role players should be carefully briefed to respond naturally, as far as possible, to the behaviour of the person undertaking the exercise.

Alternatively, an introductory phase can be used in which students should be asked to work alone, spending time (perhaps 5–10 minutes) identifying a real-world situation where their behaviour is not what they would like: maybe it lacks assertiveness, maybe they feel their reaction to a certain incident is excessive or lacks control, etc. Whatever the scenario they wish to explore, the exercise will offer them a chance to try out different ways of dealing with it.

The main phase would then require individual students (in turn), to explain their scenario to the group in order that mini role plays can be set up which re-create the incident and allow the student to try out different levels of behaviour.

They might run through the scenario attempting a more assertive approach, they may want to try a more sensitive approach; to utilize better listening or communication skills or they may wish to try to manage a challenging workplace conflict which they failed to do in the past. The important thing is that they, with the help of the group and the facilitator, consider and experiment with an array of alternative behaviours to discover which feels right for them.

Feedback advice

Feedback should be ongoing and relevant to the learning taking place at that time. A key ingredient should be a continuous review of just how realistic proposed changes of behaviour are for the student in question. There is little point in exploring alternative ways of behaving in a given incident if those proposed alternatives stand no chance of ever becoming transferred to the student's real world.

6. Best Laid Plans

Time guide: 45 minutes

Participants: Whole group

Equipment and resources:
'Best Laid Plans' worksheet

Application:
Equal opportunities training
Staff development training
Management training
Interpersonal skills training
Assertiveness training
Quality of service training

Category:
Course closure

Aim

This is a course closure exercise which encourages the student to examine personal action plans, strategies, ideas and solutions developed on the course in the light of such issues as personal commitment, spheres of influence and personal ability to influence. While this exercise has a similar theme to 'Reactions of Others' (see p. 194) its focus is different in that it seeks to explore the personal sphere.

Issues raised by this exercise

Personal development, learning through reflection.

Method

You should hand each student a 'Best Laid Plans' worksheet and ask them to read through it carefully. Clarify any aspect of it they don't fully understand or have difficulty with.

You should also explain the aim of the exercise and the importance of getting to grips with barriers to the application of learning. After all, if learning does not become transferred to action in the students' real world it negates the effectiveness of the course to encourage long-lasting and useful learning.

Each student should then work through the worksheet on their own and should be encouraged to note their reactions for future reference.

Once this phase is complete it is your choice as to how the groups should be shaped for publishing the results. You may feel it appropriate for students to work in pairs, or maybe in small groups. A whole group session may prove a bit confronting and less safe than these former two options, but which you choose will depend on how the course has gone generally and how well the students are working with each other at this point.

Variation

There needn't be a publishing phase and students could be left to make what use they will of the responses they have noted.

Feedback advice

This exercise is a reflective course closure exercise and as such does not require a separate feedback session over and above a publishing phase.

WORKSHEET

Best laid plans

Spend some time carefully thinking through the learning you feel you have gained from the course and any changes it has prompted you to make or consider making. Chances are that as the course has unfolded, you will have developed new ways of thinking about and dealing with everyday issues, problems and experiences; you may have developed strategies, solutions and new approaches and ways of acting and behaving.

Having invested time and effort in the course, it's now important that you get the best chance to put the things you have learned into practice by applying them in your real world. Before this can happen, you should give some thought to how easy it will be to apply these changes and new learning.

Work through the questions below; these will provide a structure for reviewing things which might get in the way in this regard.

Questions

How committed do you feel towards putting what you have learned on this course to use in your real world?

What things may get in the way of this commitment?

Do you have any plans to review how much of this learning you have implemented in a few months' time?

Do any of the new ways of dealing with problems and issues require you to influence the behaviour of others?

What is your ability to influence in such situations?

If you have developed a personal action plan, is it realistic?

Do you think you will implement it in full or just in part?

What might stop you implementing it in full or in part?

How different is your behaviour likely to be outside of this course when compared to the way you have behaved while a student on the course?

What influences this change?

7. Best manager

Time guide: 45 minutes–1 hour

Participants: 15–20

Equipment and resources:
Flipchart and marker or similar appropriate writing material; 'Best Manager' character traits list

Application:
Interpersonal skills training
Management training
Quality of service training

Category:
Encouraging learning through openness (attitudes, feelings)

Aim

To encourage students to explore what makes a good manager by identifying those characteristics which they would want in a good manager.

Issues raised by this exercise

Management style, interpersonal skills.

Method

Start off by explaining the basic aim of the exercise to your students.

The group should be split into smaller working teams of six to eight people and each small group provided with a piece of flipchart paper and a marker or a similar writing facility. They should be asked to draw a vertical line down the flipchart so that the paper is divided in half. One half should be labelled 'Best Manager', the other 'Worst Manager'.

Each group should be given the 'Best Manager' character traits list and asked to read it through and clarify any terms they are not familiar with. They should be then asked to complete the task by listing under 'Best Manager' those characteristics they think make for a good manager and under 'Worst Manager', those traits they think make for a poor manager.

You should explain that there is no need to ensure the lists balance. However, students might be tasked to be prepared to explain their choices at a later stage.

Before moving into a feedback phase, you should facilitate a short publishing phase during which the group re-forms and publishes its work to the larger group, clarifying points of ambiguity. They should not be asked to explain their choices at this time.

Feedback advice

Draw out differences between groups and explore their significance. Throughout, it is useful to explore what students understood by the term 'best manager': 'Best in what way?' might be an appropriate question. Did any of the groups include contradictory elements and if so how do they reconcile these?

CHARACTER TRAITS LIST

Best manager

Makes decisions
Commands respect
Consultative
Always stopping by and checking up
Works alone
Seeks advice
Orthodox
Young
Supportive
Task-centred
Leaves you to get on with things
Doesn't interfere
Pragmatic
Rarely seen
Autocratic
Approachable

Keeps his/her distance
Demands respect
Leads from the front
Works by the rules
People-centred
Bold
Makes unpopular decisions
Cynical of change
Works team hard
Asks to be kept informed
Always in his/her office
Ambitious
Mature
Time-centred
Radical
Cautious

8. Beyond disclosure

Time guide: 1 hour

Participants: 20 maximum

Equipment and resources:
'Beyond Disclosure' worksheet

Application:
Equal opportunities training
Staff development training
Management training
Interpersonal skills training
Assertiveness training
Quality of service training

Category:
Encouraging learning through openness (attitudes, feelings)

Aim

To provide a means by which students can work through a structured and sequenced reflection of their own stated attitudes on a given theme or issue, in a supportive and non-threatening way.

Issues raised by this exercise

Learning through reflection, disclosure and consideration of the consequences of holding certain attitudes and values.

Method

It is important to note that this exercise can only be used following phases in the course during which students have been encouraged to identify where they stand on a given issue or topic. This is because, as the title suggests, this exercise aims to take the student beyond such initial disclosure.

Phase 1

Ask each student to spend five minutes working alone, thinking about the course and the things about themselves (perhaps opinions, attitudes, views or beliefs) they have learned or may have disclosed to others.

They should be asked to choose one such disclosure to work with.

Explain the aim of the exercise to the group and split them into pairs. Give each participant a worksheet. Tell the group that the two students in each pair will take it in turns to be the facilitator.

Phase 2

The second phase starts when the subject informs the facilitator of the disclosure to be worked through. The facilitator, once they are satisfied they understand the disclosure, then leads the subject through the worksheet.

It is important that the student taking on the role of the facilitator understands the following things about their role:

- Their job is to encourage the subject to work through their disclosure by considering and responding to the questions posed in the worksheet. Such encouragement should involve sensitivity, good listening, encouraging non-verbal and verbal behaviour and an absence of value judgement.
- There is no rush and the facilitator should allow the subject time to think about and respond to a question when asked.
- The facilitator should not pressure the subject into answering a question they are uncomfortable with.
- The questions in the worksheet are a guide and seek to provide a framework only; they do not preclude the facilitator asking other relevant questions as long as those questions are appropriate and useful to the subject.
- Facilitators should remember that they will in turn become subjects and that their behaviour should reflect this. In other words they should act as they might wish others to behave when it is their turn to work through their own disclosure.

Feedback advice

Feedback should emphasize how important it is to go beyond disclosure to a point at which learners can begin the process of addressing or resolving what has been disclosed, to uncover consequences and to begin to develop strategies and recipes for action and change.

WORKSHEET

Beyond disclosure

For this session you will be working with a partner and together you will take it in turns to act as a facilitator while the other person works through the task by responding to questions you, as the facilitator, will ask. These questions appear below.

When you are acting as the facilitator you should make every effort to support and encourage your partner in the task. Your job is as an enabler and this should involve good listening skill, sensitivity and support. Only intervene in your partner's responses if you are quite certain you will assist their efforts.

When it is your turn to work through the questions, try to be as honest and as open as you can; in this way you will get the most from the exercise. If you are asked a question you cannot and don't want to answer, discuss this with your partner or the facilitator.

QUESTIONS

How do you feel about holding the viewpoint you have disclosed?

What do you think other people's reactions to this viewpoint might be?

What are the consequences for you of holding this disclosed viewpoint?

How compatible is this viewpoint with a commitment to equal opportunities and fair treatment?

How would you respond if challenged that this view is wrong or invalid?

How would you challenge this view for yourself?

Do you want to change this view?

What might get in the way of you changing this view?

Will anyone support you in your attempts to change?

How easy is it going to be to change this viewpoint and the behaviour which is associated with it?

9. Birthdays

Time guide:
15 minutes or more depending on why you are using it

Participants:
Any number, but the more the merrier

Equipment and resources:
A clear working space in the room

Application:
Equal opportunities training
Interpersonal skills training
Management training
Staff development training
Quality of service training

Category:
Ice-breaker
Energizer

Aim

To re-energize the group after a break.

Issues raised by this exercise

Non-verbal communication, noticing and interpreting, and group dynamics.

Method

This is a fun exercise which will help to re-energize a group and also raise some issues if required.

Announce the purpose of the exercise and then brief the participants that they are to arrange themselves in order of their birthday (not age) in a line. They may not speak or write anything down. All communication must be done non-verbally.

When they have finished ask them to sit down and then give feedback.

Variations

An alternative is to ask the participants to arrange themselves in order of how far they have to travel home from the course.

To make the non-verbal communication focus on facial expression you could also ban the use of gestures with the hands and arms.

Other variations are limited only by your imagination!

Feedback advice

This exercise can be usefully used for stimulating a discussion on the interpretation of non-verbal communication. Questions which will help include:

'How easy was it to communicate with each other?'
'Did anyone interpret signals wrongly?'
'What did such an exercise do for the group in terms of relationships?'

10. THE BLACK CAT EXERCISE

Time guide: 30 minutes

Participants: 15–20

Equipment and resources:
'The Black Cat Exercise' prompt sheet

Application:
Interpersonal skills training
Management training
Staff development training
Quality of service training

Category: Energizer

Aim

This is a light-hearted and lively energizer which encourages students to identify elements of interpersonal skill and assertiveness. The ideas generated are likely to be useful mainly as a way into the subject and as such this exercise is best used early on in a learning course

Issues raised by this exercise

Listening skills, verbal and non-verbal skills, sensitivity, assertiveness skills and conflict management skills.

Method

This exercise is based on the colloquial expression, 'a black-cat attitude' which is used to describe people who, no matter what you tell them you have, they have something better; no matter what things you may have done they have always done something bigger, better, more daring, more expensive, etc. As the saying goes, no matter how black your cat is their cat is blacker.

Split the group into small groups of three and hand each student a prompt sheet. Explain the idea of the black cat attitude and tell them that the idea of the exercise is to use this idea to explore aspects of interpersonal skill. The exercise runs in rounds, each topic on the prompt sheet representing one round. Each student in the group should take it in turns to lead a round.

The exercise is simple: the person leading the round reads the topic he/she is to start and says, 'I know a person with such good (subject area being discussed) that he/she...'; the next person then has to go one better by saying, 'that's nothing, I know a person who has such good (subject area being discussed) that he/she...'; finally, the first person tries to go one better. For example, if the topic is good listening skills the leader of the round might start by saying, 'I have a friend with good listening skills, she always seems to encourage me to tell her things' and so on and so forth until the subject has gone right round.

It is vital that students stick to the wording as given on the prompt sheet and that they don't become silly in their responses. The exercise is all about investigating interpersonal skills, assertiveness and conflict management and the group should be encouraged to stick to these subject areas.

This should be a lively and enjoyable short session which aims to energize the group and offers a quick change of pace.

Feedback advice

As this is an energizer, feedback may not be appropriate; however, if you find while monitoring the group that valuable learning is coming out that you don't want to lose, you could consider running a quick feedback session during which you inform the group of what you saw and heard.

PROMPT SHEET

Black cat exercise

Good listening skills

Sensitive to situations and people

Assertive

Good at dealing with conflict

Good communication skills

Empathetic

Works well in a team

Good attitude to equal opportunities

Non-prejudiced

11. Bust that myth!

Time guide: 1–2 hours

Participants: All group sizes

Equipment and resources:
Resource pages supplied with this exercise

Application:
Equal opportunities training
Interpersonal skills training
Assertiveness training
Staff development

Category:
Simulation and/or role play
Encouraging learning through openness (attitudes,feelings)

Aim

For students to generate their own responses to the variety of myths which spring from prejudice and/or ignorance.

Issues raised by this exercise

Stereotyping, prejudice, labelling and information to dispel myths.

Method

This exercise is best done in small groups but can also be done individually if that suits the numbers or circumstances better.

The resource pages we have supplied show myths you might want to work with in four distinct areas. You will probably have your own ideas in this respect and since this learning must be relevant, significant and meaningful to your learners you will want to include any of the myths they have generated themselves which are not given on the resource sheets. We have left space for them to add their own.

Introduce the aim of the exercise.

Decide which area you are covering (sexism, racism, disability, sexual orientation). You may want to involve the group in this decision, but this will depend on the objectives of the training.

Facilitate a discussion to draw out what some of the more common myths are in relation to the area you have decided to cover.

If the students generate their own myths and these are to be dealt with, add these to the resource sheets. Be aware that if too many are tackled, this exercise could go on for a very long time!

Ask the students to form groups or work individually (depending on what you have decided). They should carefully consider each myth, and generate as many ideas as possible to counter it. These ideas should be written down.

Time allocated for group work will depend on how many myths are being dealt with, but ten minutes to think about, discuss and write down responses for each myth is about right.

There should then be a plenary session to share the ideas generated. You may wish to record the ideas in a way that everyone can see. Learners may wish to make a note of things they have not thought of.

Variations

To avoid this session being too 'academic' and dry, why not invite students to role play? This could be done by giving each student a card with a myth on. They circulate in the room and confront each other. One of them will express the myth, and the other will present the argument against it. Continue until all the myths have been dealt with, then feedback in a plenary session as above.

Feedback advice

Feedback will centre on the ideas generated by the participants. To run this session effectively you will need to have thought through your own ideas and drawn up your own answers to the myths.

For further information you could refer to publications such as *The Equal Opportunities Guide* (Clements and Spinks, 1994, published by Kogan Page).

RESOURCE PAGE

Bust that myth!

Racist myths

Myth

'I freely admit I'm a racist, I was born that way.'

Myth

'There is little, if any, racism in this country, it's all hype!'

Myth

'Minority ethnic groups are racist themselves; they keep their culture and language and make no attempt to integrate into our culture.'

Myth

'They should go back to where they came from.'

Myth

'Britain should be kept for the British.'

RESOURCE PAGE

Bust that myth!

Sexist myths

Myth

'Women are worse drivers than men.'

Myth

'A woman's place is in the home.'

Myth

'It doesn't matter if I say chairman instead of chair, you know what I mean and in any case being politically correct is just nonsense.'

Myth

'There is such a thing as women's work and men's work.'

RESOURCE PAGE

Bust that myth!

Myths about people with a disability

Myth

'Deaf people shouldn't work on building sites because they can't hear warnings.'

Myth

'There is a link between intelligence and clarity of speech.'

Myth

'People in wheelchairs cannot speak for themselves.'

RESOURCE PAGE

Bust that myth!

Myths about sexual orientation

Myth

'You can tell a person's sexuality by the way they dress.'

Myth

'Homosexuality is an illness.'

Myth

'Gay men are effeminate, lesbians are butch.'

12. Challenge escalation

Time guide: 1–1.5 hours

Participants:
Any size group but works best with ten or more

Equipment and resources:
Resource page provided with this exercise

Application:
Equal opportunities training
Interpersonal skills training
Management training
Staff development training
Assertiveness training
Quality of service training

Category:
Simulation and/or role play
Encouraging learning through openness (attitudes, feelings)

Aim

To practise the use of assertiveness skills in increasingly difficult situations, and identify coping strategies.

Issues raised by this exercise

Assertiveness; identifying the difficulties of challenging inappropriate behaviour and attitudes.

Method

Announce the purpose of the exercise to the group.

Arrange for the participants to split into pairs and explain that for the first stage they will work together and then swap roles. For stages two and three of the exercise they should be encouraged to change partners.

Level 1

Issue one person in each pair with the first scenario of level 1. Their job is to make the assertion to their partner, whose role it is then to challenge the assertion. About five minutes should be allowed for each assertion and challenge. When the first challenge has been made the partners should swap roles and use the second scenario for level 1.

After this has taken place gather the groups together for feedback (see feedback advice below). Your aim as facilitator should be to identify what the participants found difficult and what they found easy. Identify the issues involved in challenging inappropriate attitudes and behaviour. Remember that the purpose of this exercise is not so much the content of the challenges but the interpersonal issues involved.

Level 2

After the first feedback ask the participants to change partners and move to level 2, which contains some harder challenges. Work through the same process.

Level 3

For level 3 you should allow the participants to set their own scenarios based on their own real-world experience. Ask the participants to think about the issues that they personally find difficult to challenge in their own work or other context. These issues should then be used as the basis for level 3. Encourage the learning which has taken place in level 1 and 2 to be put into practice.

Variations

Although this exercise is principally aimed at challenging inappropriate behaviour and attitudes, you could also use it as a framework or vehicle to discover the issues involved in other types of difficult interactions. Issues which could be dealt with by this exercise include;

Breaking bad news
Giving difficult appraisals
Saying no to customers
Saying no to managers
Saying no to staff
Saying no to people who expect you to say yes.

Feedback advice

This exercise is one which is likely to generate a great deal of discussion because most people in our experience find it difficult to challenge attitudes and behaviour.

During the feedback of level 1 and 2 the following trigger questions may be useful to get you going:

'What sorts of challenges were made ... what were the issues?'
'What were the three most difficult things about making the challenge?'
'What sorts of emotions were you experiencing when you were challenging?'
'On reflection, would anyone have challenged differently?'
'What feelings did the people challenged experience?'
'Can we generate a set of guidelines about challenging which would be useful and actually work in the real-world?'

RESOURCE PAGE

Challenge escalation

Challenges for level 1

A. Both participants to read

You are both in a canteen or staff restaurant. While queuing for a meal, the challenger overhears the person to be challenged tell a racist joke. Having been on an equal opportunities course just recently, and knowing that the organization has a strong equal opportunities policy, the challenger decides to do something about this behaviour by confronting the person making the joke.

B. Both participants to read

You find a colleague about to put some nude pin-ups on a wall where you know they will be seen by female colleagues.

Challenges for level 2

A.

A colleague insists in a discussion that AIDS is a gay plague. When challenged he gets very irritated.

B.

You are with a friend in the office and you both own computers at home. No one else is about and your office has just had a delivery of floppy disks. He tells you that he is taking some and offers you a box, saying that no one will notice if you help yourselves.

13. Challenge identification

Time guide: 1 hour

Participants: Nine or more

Equipment and resources:
A selection of challenges and an observer's score sheet supplied for this exercise

Application:
Equal opportunities training
Interpersonal skills training
Management training
Staff development training

Category:
Simulation and/or role play
Encouraging learning through openness (attitudes, feelings)

Aim

To encourage the learners to identify different types of challenge, and to recognize that sensitive challenging is usually the most effective strategy.

Issues raised by this exercise

Interpersonal skill, sensitivity, prejudice and discrimination and management skill.

Method

Announce the purpose of the exercise to the group and explain that there are many different ways of challenging, and sensitive challenging is the usually most appropriate.

Arrange for the participants to split into threes and explain that two people will work together with one observer (with a score sheet) and then they will swap roles. This will continue until all the challenges are exhausted.

Each group should have a list of challenges, which are either:

I notice you just said....
or
I notice you just ... (did something)

The first member of the team takes the first issue on the list and says to their partner, 'I notice you just said (or did)...' They should go on to challenge the words or behaviour and their partner should defend themselves.

After two minutes, they should stop.

The observer then rates the challenge out of ten on several dimensions (see the observer's score sheet), shows the challenger the score and justifies, with examples, the mark they have awarded.

The group changes role and carries on with the next challenge.

Variations

We have given a selection of challenges for you to use. You can vary this exercise by writing your own challenges or getting the participants to write their own, to suit their real-world issues and problems.

Feedback advice

The scores each challenger achieved are not important. The score sheet should, however, stimulate discussion.

When the groups have finished, questions which will help stimulate further discussion are broadly the same as for the exercise in challenge escalation; these include:

'What sorts of challenges were made ... what were the issues?'
'What were the most difficult things about making the challenge?'
'What sorts of emotions were you experiencing when you were challenging?'
'On reflection would anyone have challenged differently?'
'What feelings did the people challenged experience?'
'Can we generate a set of guidelines about challenging which would be useful and actually work in the real world?'
'What types of challenge were most successful?'

A SELECTION OF CHALLENGES

Challenge identification

I notice you just said ... that it would be better if all black people went home.

I notice you just said ... that women should see themselves as primarily for childbirth.

I notice you just said ... there are many jobs women cannot do.

I notice you just said ... it's well know that Arabs are liars.

I notice you just said ... disabled people are a nuisance on public transport.

I notice you just said ... gay men are always effeminate.

I notice you just said ... AIDS would not be a problem but for gay people.

I notice you just ... ignored a black colleague when he spoke to you.

I notice you just ... told a racist joke.

I notice you just ... told a sexist joke.

I notice you just ... chose a white candidate when you knew a black candidate had better qualifications.

I notice you just ... took the mickey out of a person with learning difficulty behind their back.

I notice you just ... pinned a nude picture on the wall where you knew female members of staff would see it and be offended.

I notice you just ... treated that customer differently; she was Asian ... all your other customers have been white.

OBSERVER'S SCORE SHEET

Challenge identification

Sensitive	1 2 3 4 5 6 7 8 9 10	Insensitive
Active	1 2 3 4 5 6 7 8 9 10	Passive
Assertive	1 2 3 4 5 6 7 8 9 10	Non-assertive
Non-aggressive	1 2 3 4 5 6 7 8 9 10	Aggressive
Penetrating	1 2 3 4 5 6 7 8 9 10	Shallow
Effective	1 2 3 4 5 6 7 8 9 10	Non-effective

14. Characteristics of a support person

Time guide: 1–1.5 hours

Participants: All group sizes

Equipment and resources:
Medium for writing where everyone can see (OHP, whiteboard, flipchart, chalkboard, etc.); resource page for this exercise

Application:
Equal opportunities training
Interpersonal skills training
Management training
Assertiveness training
Staff development
Quality of service

Category:
Encouraging learning through openness (attitudes, feelings)
Course closure

Aim

To help students identify the type of person they could rely on to support them in the face of pressure to conform to negative influences within an organization.

Issues raised by this exercise

Values and attitudes, peer pressure, stereotyping and integrity.

Method

Phase 1

Brainstorm. Open the session by brainstorming all the things the learners can think of which might cause them difficulty in carrying out their work in ways which their personal values dictate or in accordance with standards set down by the organization.

The sorts of things which we anticipate are likely to come up are: pressure to conform to the 'sub-culture' which legitimizes taking short cuts, racism or sexism, not valuing the customer in any real sense, dishonesty and so on.

Write the suggestions of the group up where all can see and reflect on them.

Facilitate a discussion about what gives rise to these things: are any members of the group willing to share any of their personal experiences? What are the real problems which they face in these respects?

Phase 2

It is likely that the discussion arising out of phase 1 will have been rather gloomy and negative, with the focus being on negative aspects of peer pressure. One of the ways of handling this is to draw on the strengths on someone in the organization who will be supportive of an ethical, straightforward or honest approach to interpreting the organization's values and goals.

Hand out the reflection sheets given with this exercise. Ask the students to complete them and be prepared to pool their ideas with the group; they should take about 10 minutes.

Ask each student in turn to share with the group what they have put and record these in a way that everyone can see.

Facilitate a discussion about what has been recorded, using the feedback advice below.

Feedback advice

'Characteristics of a support person' makes an excellent course closure activity. This is particularly so when the participants have generated lots of good ideas about appropriate attitudes, best practice, giving quality service or sensitive management, but as the comfortable, safe environment of the courseroom is soon to pass, anxiety can set in about how to stand by what has been learned.

This exercise can easily turn into a no-hope, whining session if you do not handle it carefully. It is all too easy to dwell on the things which are difficult or negative and gain the sense that there is really nothing we can do about it so we all might as well go home. The aim of the session is to be positive and to learn that one very positive thing which *can* be done is to identify people in your organization who are ideal role models and whose characteristics are such that they will support newer members of an organization or institution. Some questions which are useful in achieving the aim include:

'Looking at the list of characteristics of a support person, which of those qualities do you think are most important?'

'How many of those qualities do you have?'
'How true is it that there is strength in numbers?'
'Who will be looking to *you* to be a good role model?'

RESOURCE PAGE

Characteristics of a support person

We are trying to identify the characteristics of a person who:

- is a good role model for the values of your organization
- you could draw on for support.

Identify as many characteristics as you can; here's a couple to get you started:

– Good listener

– Approachable

–

–

–

–

–

–

–

15. Consequences

Time guide: 1 hour

Participants: Any size group

Equipment and resources:
Resource page provided with this exercise; flipchart paper; broad nibbed pens

Application:
Equal opportunities training
Management training
Staff development training
Quality of service training

Category:
Encouraging learning through openness (attitudes, feelings)

Aim

To identify and explore the consequences of both personal and institutional prejudice, discrimination and labelling for minority groups.

Issues raised by this exercise

Prejudice, discrimination, attitudes and values, labelling and stereotyping.

Method

Announce the aim for the exercise.

Divide the participants into groups of about four and issue each with a card made up from the resource page for this exercise and a sheet of flipchart paper and pen.

Instruct each group that they should focus entirely on the consequences of:

Prejudice
Discrimination
Stereotyping/labelling

for the groups they have been given.

These should be shown as three columns on the flipchart, with one piece of flipchart paper for each minority group dealt with.

Feedback advice

This exercise is very useful in situations where learners insist that prejudice and discrimination is not a real problem. Your learners will identify a large number of the consequences for minority groups and you will then be able to use this information for a wider discussion about the personal and institutional consequences of prejudice, discrimination and stereotyping.

RESOURCE PAGE

Consequences

Black people	Asian people	People in wheelchairs
Hindus	Muslims	Deaf people
Christians	Jews	Old people
Gay men	Lesbians	Blind people
Gypsies	New Age travellers	Women

16. Constructing stereotypes

Time guide: 1.5 hours

Participants: Any size group

Equipment and resources:
Resource page provided with this exercise; a quantity of flipchart paper; broad nibbed pens; tape to post the flipchart

Application:
Equal opportunities training
Interpersonal skills training
Management training
Staff development training
Quality of service training

Category:
Encouraging learning through openness (attitudes, feelings)

Aim

For the participants to understand the nature of stereotyping and to identify ways in which some minority groups are sometimes stereotyped.

Issues raised by this exercise

Stereotyping, labelling, prejudice, discrimination and treating people as individuals.

Method

This exercise has a wide application because by its very nature stereotyping applies to nearly all spheres of life.

Announce the purpose of the exercise and arrange for the learners to get into mixed groups of three.

Each group should be issued with as many sheets of flipchart as assignments they will be asked to do (probably about four). They should also be given a broad nibbed pen.

Issue each group with a set of four 'stereotype cards' (the same to each group) which you can make up by photocopying the resource page, cutting up the sheets and sticking them onto card. (You could just use the paper if you prefer, since you can photocopy the resource page as many times as you like.)

Each group then has about seven minutes per card to try and construct a stereotype of the groups they have been given. They should note as bullet points on the flipchart all the ways in which they believe that the group is stereotyped either by them or others. It's important that you allow the participants to use what they believe to be other people's perceptions, as in some groups the participants may refuse to do the exercise at all, claiming that they hold no stereotypes. If this does happen then deal with it in feedback.

When the groups have finished, post each set of stereotypes alongside each other so that you can help the group compare them.

Facilitate a discussion along the lines given in the feedback section below.

Feedback advice

Refer back to the aim of the exercise and also make use of the feedback advice given in Chapter 3 of this binder.

Key questions which will help achieve the aim include:

'Identify which of the stereotyping is negative and which positive. Why do you think the balance is as it is?'

'What are the strengths of stereotyping and what are its dangers?'

'How does stereotyping lead to prejudice and discrimination?'

'What were the sources for the ideas we put up in each group? How many of the things were from our own direct experience?'

'What strategies could we adopt to avoid such stereotyping?'

RESOURCE PAGE

Constructing stereotypes

Black people	Asian people	People in wheelchairs
Hindus	Muslims	Buddhists
Christians	Jews	Old people
Gay men	Lesbians	Punks
Gypsies	New Age travellers	Skinheads

17. Cultural objects

Time guide:
1 hour (depending on the number of students)

Participants: Any size group

Equipment and resources:
An article which evokes for the participant the culture which is being discussed; chairs arranged in a circle around a low table; briefing sheet given as the resource page for this exercise

Application:
Equal opportunities training
Quality of service training

Category:
Encouraging learning through openness (attitudes, feelings)

Aim

To help students understand the diverse nature of culture, and to recognize that some images of culture can be misleading and exclusionary.

Issues raised by this exercise

Stereotyping and prejudice, ideas about the nature of culture, nationalism, labelling, the rich variety of culture and multiculturalism.

Method

This exercise is far more effective if participants are briefed some time before the event. They will need to bring with them an article which evokes for them the culture under discussion. Use the briefing note which is supplied in the resource page for this exercise.

If British culture is what is being reviewed then they would be asked to bring an object which speaks to them of Britain. Examples from our own experience include stamps bearing the Queen's head (hence the monarchy), a postcard showing a cricket match on a village green, and a box of liquorice allsorts which to the person who brought them spoke of diversity.

Participants sit in a circle around a low table such as a coffee table. Each student in turn is asked to place their object on the table and the group can reflect for a moment on why that particular object might evoke the culture in question. Then the student who placed it is asked to explain why they chose it.

Variations

Students can be asked to bring objects to evoke different cultures, perhaps a different culture each. This will broaden the discussion to issues about stereotyping and labelling.

Feedback advice

As with most exercises of this nature the feedback stage is critical. In our experience the act of teasing out from your participants why they chose the article in question will tend to stimulate a discussion and you will need to decide whether to cut this short and discuss it fully at the end or to go with it at the time and get the most from it then. It is quite likely that you will choose the latter as it seems to be more spontaneous.

Questions which will help achieve the aim include:

'To what extent might this object be a false image of the culture in question?'
'What qualifies something to be British?'
'What processes may have been operating to influence your choice?'

RESOURCE PAGE

Cultural objects

Briefing notes to be given out in advance of the exercise

You will be taking part in an exercise to discover as much as we can about culture and the extent to which there really is such a thing as a 'pure culture'. You are asked to:

- Bring to the session an object (preferably not too large!) which speaks to you of . . . culture.
- Be prepared to explain to the group why the object you have chosen evokes the culture you have been asked to represent.

18. Draw what you think

Time guide: 15 minutes to 1 hour

Participants: Any sized group

Equipment and resources:
Flipchart for each group; broad nibbed pens; tape to post the flipchart on the wall

Application:
Equal opportunities training
Interpersonal skills training
Management training
Staff development training
Quality of service training

Category:
Energizer
Encouraging learning through openness (attitudes, feelings)

Aim

To encourage participants to give expression to difficult concepts through the medium of drawing.

Issues raised by this exercise

Understanding and disclosure of attitudes and feelings about a variety of issues.

Method

This exercise has been found very useful as a quick session to energize a group and help it find its way again, or as a set piece where the issues dealt with (and drawn) are planned and thought through.

Announce that the purpose of the exercise is to try and understand or define an issue by drawing it.

Divide the group into smaller units – three or four to each unit is about right.

If you are working with a particular issue which has come up in your course then obviously that will be the one you ask your participants to capture by drawing it.

Example: Say the issue you are exploring is what it feels like to confront someone who has just told a racist joke. Ask the groups to draw images of all the things that this situation implies – the feelings involved, the personalities involved, the attitudes revealed and so on. They can be as free as they wish and should be encouraged to use colour. You will find it surprising just how creative your learners will be.

If you are doing the set piece exercise, then issue each group with one or more of the briefing sheets provided for this exercise.

Variations

Another medium which your learners could use is plasticine. This is inexpensive and easily used, and will provide some interesting results.

Feedback advice

Post the resultant flipchart on the wall and then ask each group in turn to explain to the others why they have drawn what they have. Concentrate on the use of colour and the significance of the images they have produced. Trigger questions might include:

'Why have you drawn your topic in this way?'
'Did you consider any alternatives?'
'Do you think others see the issue in this way?'
'Was there any debate in your group about what you would draw?'
'What are the positive images and what are the negative?'
'What gives rise to these?'

RESOURCE PAGE

Draw what you think

- Your group has been provided with a flipchart and a variety of pens.
- Being as creative as you wish, and making full use of colour, draw an image or series of images which express:

The negative aspects of sexism

The negative aspects of racism

The ways in which the environment can disable people

The difficulty of challenging inappropriate behaviour

Attitudes towards lesbians and men who are gay

The values of the organization to which you belong

19. Faulty goods

Time guide: 1 hour

Participants: Six or more

Equipment and resources:
Resource page provided with this exercise; items of faulty goods for return (eg, a pair of child's trousers, a broken tennis racquet, a chipped mug or a pen that won't write); furniture suitable to simulate a shop counter

Application:
Interpersonal skills training
Management training
Staff development training
Assertiveness training
Quality of service training

Category:
Simulation and/or role play
Encouraging learning through openness (attitudes, feelings)

Aim

To explore the issues raised in confronting a difficult situation and to practise skills of assertiveness and negotiation.

Issues raised by this exercise

Assertive behaviour, confronting and noticing and interpreting non-verbal behaviour.

Method

This exercise exploits a common scenario with a wide application to a variety of types of training. More will be said about this in the feedback.

We are assuming here that you have some experience of role play and will be familiar with concepts of detailed briefing, setting up the role play, negotiating with the role players and arranging to de-role the participants afterwards if necessary.

Identify the role players and brief them using the resource page provided with this exercise.

Run the role play and feedback as below.

After the first feedback session you might consider it a good idea to summarize the learning points and then run the role play again, giving a fresh set of participants the opportunity to put into practice what has been learned.

Feedback advice

Your feedback must be adapted to fit the application for your training. One way of doing this will be to concentrate on the *issues* raised by having to return faulty goods rather than having any discussion about the actual act of returning things. The sorts of issues (presented in the form of questions) which will need to be discussed are:

'What sorts of things were going through the minds of the sales assistant and the returner at the following stages of the role play?'
- before they had met?
- when they actually met?
- during their discussion?
- after the discussion?

'What non-verbal communication was noticed at these stages?'
'What interpretation can be placed on the non-verbal communication?'
'Was the counter used in any way by the participants?'
'How correct were the interpretations?' (Check with the participants.)
'What gets in the way of our being assertive?'
'What are the differences between assertiveness and aggressiveness?'
'Who held the power in the role play?'
'Can we identify parallel situations where we work?'
'How are these normally dealt with? Could they be dealt with differently?'

BRIEFING FOR ROLE PLAYERS

Faulty goods

Scenario:
The room has been set up as a shop. There is a counter and there are two people involved in this situation.

Sales Assistant
You are a fairly junior member of staff and are serving alone. There is no manager available at the moment for you to call on. You have been told that under no circumstances are refunds to be given without reference to a manager.

Customer (returning goods)
You visited this shop yesterday and bought (whatever object your facilitator has arranged). Whatever the object is, it either does not work, has shrunk (child's trousers can provide a striking representation of adult trousers which have shrunk!) or in some other way is faulty.

You have returned to the shop. You want your money back, not a replacement item, you want it now, and you don't want excuses from the sales assistant.

20. Find someone who . . .

Time guide: 20 minutes

Participants:
10 or more (doesn't work very well with less)

Equipment and resources:
Resource sheet provided with this exercise

Applications:
Equal opportunities training
Interpersonal skills training
Management training
Assertiveness training
Staff development training
Quality of service training

Category:
Ice-breaker
Energizer

Aim

To introduce participants to each other, get them talking and start the process of opening up to each other.

Issues raised by this exercise

None, unless the categories chosen are emotive (see below).

Method

Introduce the aim of the exercise.

Hand out an exercise sheet and something to write with to each participant.

Instruct participants to mingle in the room, and make sure they speak to everybody. You may have to help this along, as we have found that when two participants find something in common, they tend to fall into conversation and forget the exercise!

Once a participant locates a person who matches a category on the sheet, they should write that person's full name in the box provided. It can often be helpful to add the requirement that the name recorded is the name that person would like to be known by within the learning group (as long as this is appropriate).

We have left two boxes blank for you to add additional categories if you wish. Alternatively, these may be left blank.

It often helps if you join in.

Variation

This exercise makes an excellent ice-breaker, particularly if you tailor-make it to the participants you are training. It makes it more fun and relevant to them and because of that seems to break the ice more readily.

A note on the categories on the grid

We generally advise that you find out as much as you can about participants before the session; we go into this in much more detail in *A Practical Guide to Facilitation Skills* (Spinks and Clements, 1993, published by Kogan Page).

In finding out about your learners you will probably come across ideas which will help you choose some categories which will be more relevant. In a preliminary meeting with a sponsor we once noted that he was wearing a badge proclaiming that he was a member of a bee-keeping association. Making a mental note of this and remembering that he would be well-known by the participants, we included this as a category. It raised some humour, he was delighted and the ice was well and truly broken.

Remember too that the categories can be used to start gently raising the issues that you intend to deal with in the training. On an HIV awareness course we attended where a similar exercise was run, one of the categories was, find a person who knows how to use a condom. Given the light-hearted atmosphere of what was ostensibly merely an ice-breaker, it became surprisingly easy to talk about what would normally be a very sensitive issue.

Feedback advice

This exercise can perform a number of functions.

If it is merely to break the ice, then feedback might be completely unnecessary. If, on the other hand, you want to start introducing more sensitive categories, it would be a good idea to spend some time talking about the issues raised. Some questions which might help include:

'How easy did you find it to mix with the other members of the group?'
'How did you decide who to speak to first?'
'How easy was it to break into other people's conversations?'
'Did you feel embarrassed by any aspect of the exercise. If you did, why?'

RESOURCE SHEET

Find...

A person who reads *The Times*	A person wearing green	A person who votes Liberal Democrat
A person wearing blue	A Labour supporter	A person who can play the piano
A person who has been to Cyprus	A person who can define 'political correctness'	A person who has an interesting hobby
A person who likes wine	A person who never uses the wrong word	A football supporter
A person who has seen the Eiffel Tower		
A person who has never been drunk	A person who found their way here easily!	A person who likes dancing

21. Future Action Challenge

Time guide: 45 minutes

Participants: 15–20

Equipment and resources:
'Future Action Challenge' worksheet

Application:
Equal opportunities training
Staff development training
Management training
Interpersonal skills training
Assertiveness training
Quality of service training

Category:
Course closure

Aim

This is a course closure exercise which seeks to encourage students to work through a structured review of the key learning arising from the course as seen from their perspective.

Issues raised by this exercise

The issues raised during this session will vary and are dependent upon matters raised by members of the learning group themselves.

Method

You should explain the broad aim of this exercise to your students, and the usefulness of identifying key learning for themselves as a means of moving forward from the course back into their real world.

Method 1

The group remains in plenary form and each student is given a 'Future Action Challenge' worksheet which they should be asked to read carefully and take time to consider fully. Allow the group about 10–15 minutes for this phase.

After careful consideration you can then facilitate a full group discussion of the findings, encouraging students to contribute as and where they see fit. At the same time, key points can be recorded on a flipchart or whiteboard to aid learning.

Method 2

Split the group into smaller groups, providing each member of each group with a worksheet. As with method 1, a period of thoughtful reflection should be encouraged before groups start to discuss the issues raised by the task.

After small group discussion you could then draw everyone together for a plenary review of the major points raised.

Feedback advice

This is by its very nature a feedback exercise, providing as it does a structured means of reviewing the course and reflecting upon key learning.

WORKSHEET

Future action challenge

Working on your own, carefully read the following question sheet. It is designed to encourage you to think about the course you have just completed and to identify what is, for you, the key learning to have come out of it. Try to answer all the questions if you can and be as honest as possible. The questions should help you to work out how best to take learning from this course back into your everyday life and use it to best effect.

You may find it useful to make notes of your responses for future reference.

What has been the most important learning on the course for you?

What parts of the course will be particularly useful to you in your real world?

How do you plan to make use of the things you have learned?

What problems or issues do you feel you have resolved on the course?

Do you consider that you have acquired new skills on this course? If so what are these skills and how will they be of use to you?

How will you ensure that the hard work you have invested in this course doesn't go to waste?

Has the course challenged or changed your viewpoint on the issues you have worked through? If so, how will this change affect your future behaviour?

22. Group rules exercise

Time guide: 30–45 minutes

Participants:
Whole group regardless of size

Equipment and resources:
'Group Rules' worksheet, flipchart and marker

Application:
Equal opportunities training
Interpersonal skills training
Management training
Staff development training
Quality of service training

Category:
Ice-breaker
Encouraging learning through openness (attitudes, feelings)

Aim

To encourage group members to identify simple and achievable rules for the group which would assist them to get the most from the course.

Issues raised by this exercise

Team building and group learning issues.

Method

The facilitator should emphasize that group members will benefit from identifying a small number of straightforward and achievable group rules which will make sense to each member.

It can assist if participants attempt to complete the statements, 'I will personally get more learning out of this course if...' and, 'The following things might get in the way of my learning....

Group rules that might emerge may include the right to talk without interruption, that group members should speak for themselves, that people should try to be honest and willing to take part, etc.

Feedback advice

It is all too easy to get bogged down in unachievable and meaningless contract setting, a fact which can easily get in the way of effective learning. Facilitators should be realistic and encourage the group to adopt only achievable and necessary rules which promise to maintain an open, honest and fair learning environment.

WORKSHEET

Group rules exercise

Think carefully about this course and what you hope to get from it personally. In order to get the most learning from the course it may be necessary to agree some simple and achievable ground rules to make sure each group member gets the most out of the time available.

Below, please write down ground rules which you think the group should adopt. Please remember that to be useful and effective such rules should be achievable, necessary and simply stated.

Ground rules

23. IDENTIFY THE LANGUAGE

Time Guide: 40 minutes

Participants: Any size group

Equipment and resources:
Resource page provided with this exercise; flipchart and broad nibbed pens; tape to post the flipchart

Application:
Equal opportunities training
Interpersonal skills training
Management training
Staff development training
Quality of service training

Category:
Encouraging learning through openness (attitudes, feelings)

Aim

To explore the notion of 'political correctness in relation to language'.

Issues raised by this exercise

Language, attitudes and values.

Method

Announce the aim of the exercise.

Issue each participant with a photocopy of the resource page, and ask them to work alone for ten minutes, identifying all the examples they can of:

Qualified language
Exclusionary language
Language which has a racist effect
Language which has a sexist effect
Language which puts gays and lesbians down
Language which might give offence to people with a disability

Then ask participants to join with a partner, and for five minutes compare notes and add omissions.

Pairs should then join into fours and do the same for five minutes.

Recall the groups to a plenary session and record the total results on a flipchart headed with the appropriate title.

Feedback advice

You may need to start with a discussion about the importance of language, who sees it as important and who doesn't. Point out that language *is* behaviour in terms of the anti-discrimination legislation and most equality policies. Then work through the examples the groups have identified and achieve consensus as to the suitability or otherwise of the language.

RESOURCE PAGE

Identify the language

Qualified language eg, lady doctor	**Exclusionary language** eg, fireman
Racist language eg, black people should go home	**Sexist language** eg, Essex girl jokes
Insensitive language to gays/ lesbians eg, poofter/dyke	**Insensitive language to disabled people/people with learning disability** eg, nutter

24. 'I'M LIKE THIS AND YOU'RE LIKE THIS'

Time guide: 60–80 minutes

Participants: Maximum 12–15

Equipment and resources:
Worksheets provided on resource page(s)

Application:
Interpersonal skills training
Management training
Staff development training
Quality of service training

Category:
Encouraging learning through openness (attitudes, feelings)

Aim

The exercise has two main aims:

1. To encourage group members to reflect upon and disclose things about themselves and how they think they come across to others, in a balanced and safe way.
2. To offer feedback to other group members by identifying those people in the group whom they think share similar strengths and similar developmental needs as themselves.

Issues raised by this exercise

Self-image, communication and feedback to others.

Method

Phase 1

The facilitator explains the aim of the exercise, issues the worksheets and introduces this individual phase of reflection and completion of worksheets.

Group members should be told to avoid writing the first ideas that occur to them but instead should spend some time thinking about and considering both the questions on the worksheet and the most honest response to them. The issue of avoidance should be mentioned.

Following completion the group should come back together again. The facilitator should then carefully explain phase 2.

Phase 2

The second phase involves group members sharing their work with each other, a process which should be directed and controlled by the facilitator, who needs to be encouraging and supportive.

Feedback advice

This is essentially a self-image and self-disclosure exercise which involves the additional element of feedback to others. The safety aspect is heightened by the fact that no student can identify something in another person that they haven't first identified about themselves.

The exercise can be used to cover a number of different topic areas such as team building and looking at the positive and not so positive aspects of day-to-day relationships within a team of people. Alternatively it could be used to examine aspects of interpersonal skill in which a member might consider their listening and communication abilities, for example.

It is important to stress the need for honesty and to encourage a degree of risk-taking in terms of both disclosing and feedback. There may also be a need to emphasize the importance of reflection, disclosure and feedback within the area of personal awareness and development.

WORKSHEET

I'm like this and you're like this

This worksheet is split into two distinct parts. Working on your own and being as honest and open as you feel you are able, you should complete the two tasks. Should you need clarification or wish to discuss this worksheet, you should speak with your facilitator before undertaking the exercise.

While this exercise asks you to identify aspects of other people's behaviour you find problematic or difficult, it has an in-built safety feature in that you cannot give feedback to others about aspects of their behaviour unless you too are prone to similar behaviour and are prepared to reveal it in yourself, hence the title, 'I'm like this and you're like this'. For example, if you think a fellow student is a poor listener, you could only say this on the worksheet if this were also true for you and you were prepared to reveal this fact to others in the group. This is equally true of positive points as well, so that not only do you give positive feedback to others but you also acknowledge it in yourself.

Self-image is an important area of self-development and is one of the main steps towards developing effective reflective practice, a skill which enables you to learn through effective reflection. One of the main barriers to reflective learning is being defensive. This exercise will help you work through feelings of defensiveness and justification.

Phase 1 (things I could improve about my attitudes or behaviour)
Think carefully about yourself and the way you deal with and react towards others. In this part of the task you are asked to identify three aspects of your behaviour you would like to change which you also recognize in others within the group. Note these things down:

Me	Other	Name
(1)	(1)	....
(2)	(2)	....
(3)	(3)	....

Phase 2 (things which I think are positive aspects of my behaviour)
Repeat phase 1 but this time focus on the positive, the things you are happy with about your attitudes and/or behaviour. Once again, you are asked to identify others whom you feel share these positive elements of behaviour or attitude.

Me	Other	Name
(1)	(1)	....
(2)	(2)	....
(3)	(3)	....

25. Inappropriate attitudes and behaviour

Time guide: 1.5 hours

Participants: 15–20

Equipment and resources:
'Inappropriate Attitudes and Behaviour' worksheet, flipchart paper and marker or similar suitable writing material

Application:
Equal opportunities training

Category:
Encouraging learning through openness (attitudes, feelings)

Aim

To encourage students to identify typical inappropriate attitudes in given topic areas and the behaviour that might be a consequence. This exercise also assists the learner to see the very real link between attitudes held and consequent behaviour.

Issues raised by this exercise

Attitudes, prejudices, discrimination and unfairness.

Method

You should start the session by running a short discussion on the possible link between a person's attitudes and opinions and their resultant behaviour. Students should be encouraged to decide for themselves whether they think there is a link between the two and if so how strong it is.

The group should be split up into a number of smaller groups of about five to six people and given the 'Inappropriate Attitudes and Behaviour' worksheet. Each student should be asked to read it through and to clarify with you any areas of confusion or misunderstanding.

The worksheet provides each group with a number of short

scenarios; students should read these and then decide what typical inappropriate attitudes may exist in this given circumstance, noting their findings.

After they have completed all the scenarios they should be tasked to move to the next phase by deciding what possible consequences holding such inappropriate attitudes might have in terms of explicit behaviour.

There should then be a publishing phase whereby each group is given a few minutes to explain their work to the larger group before moving on to feedback.

Variations

Alternatively, the groups could take it in turns to role play the explicit behaviours they have identified as being possibly the consequences of a given inappropriate attitude, this with a view to encouraging observers from other groups to suggest what underlying attitudes such behaviour may give voice to.

Feedback advice

The main purpose of this exercise is to illustrate the strong link between the attitudes we hold and our observable behaviour. Too often, people argue that they should be allowed to think what they like as long as they control those views and do not let them affect their behaviour.

WORKSHEET

Inapropriate attitudes and behaviour

A taxi with its 'for hire' sign lit is driving down a busy street in the West End of London at 5pm. A passer-by sees the cab driver turn to look as a black man tries to hail him down in good time; the passer-by sees a white man a few yards further on also hailing the same cab. The taxi drives past the black man but stops and collects the white passenger.

A group is talking together at a party when one of the men in the group says, 'Yes, my wife told me she fancied going back to work but when she learned I wasn't in favour of it she soon shelved that idea.'

A woman serving at a café is waiting on tables when she notices that a man, seated in a wheelchair eating lunch with a woman, drops his knife. She walks over, replaces the knife and says to the woman, 'Poor thing' and nods in the direction of the man.

Two personnel managers are talking over a cup of coffee when one says to the other, 'I do get a lot of Asian women apply for sales assistant jobs but I can't help them because they'll frighten off trade and damage business.'

26. In-group, out-group

Time guide: 45 minutes–1 hour

Participants: 15–20

Equipment and resources:
'In-group, Out-group' worksheet provided in resource page(s)

Application:
Equal opportunities training

Category:
Encouraging learning through openness (attitudes, feelings)

Aim

To examine student experiences (and perhaps membership) of 'in' groups and 'out' groups, their characteristics, behaviour, attitudes to each other and consequences. The exercise will also help to stimulate learning about the effects of prejudice and discrimination and may also raise the issue of power.

Issues raised by this exercise

Prejudice and discrimination, power and its effects and the consequences of exclusionary behaviour.

Method

Explain the exercise aim to the group. Split the group up as appropriate. Clearly explain whether a group is to consider 'in' group situations, 'out' group situations, or both.

Ask groups to think about their experiences of such groups by responding to the questions posed in the 'In-group, Out-group' worksheet.

Movement back into plenary session will assist the facilitator to gather in the work done in the smaller groups and to undertake a more general consideration of the findings of all learners. This is especially necessary if certain groups have been working on either in-group or out-group issues only.

Variations

Depending on the time you have available you might like to consider allowing groups to respond to those questions on the worksheet that are most relevant to them or by tasking different groups to work on different parts of the worksheet so that the whole group covers the worksheet.

Feedback advice

Allow plenty of time for the group to both publish and work through their responses. Try and focus discussions on the relevance of issues raised to everyday relationships and problems. It can be useful to encourage students to consider the consequences of the behaviours and attitudes they have identified for people who find themselves on either side of the in-group, out-group divide.

WORKSHEET

In-group, out-group

In-group only

Working in your team, your task is to note down ways in which in-groups maintain their identity and membership, how they deal with attempts by others to enter their group, how they view people who are in out-groups and how they keep such people out.

Once you have done this try answering the following questions:

What does it feel like to be a member of the in-group?

How are members of the in-group known to each other?

How is membership sustained?

Why is the in-group's shared identity important?

How does the in-group view members of the out-group?

How does the in-group deal with having to accommodate out-group individuals entering the group?

Out-group only

Working in your team, your task is to note down what it is like to be a member of an out-group looking at the in-group from the outside. What do members of the in-group do to keep you out? How are you likely to react to the way in which they maintain their membership of and identity within the in-group? What would you have to do to gain entry into the in-group, if this is even possible?

Once you have done this try answering the following questions:

What is it like to be on the outside looking in?

Who holds the power and what is that power?

What would it mean to you if you couldn t gain entry to the in-group?

If you did gain entry, how would people you left behind in the out-group view you?

27. Interview pair questionnaire

Time guide:
20 minutes for each pair of people in the group

Participants: Any size group

Equipment and resources:
Resource pages supplied with this exercise

Application:
Equal opportunities training
Interpersonal skills training
Management training
Staff development training
Quality of service training

Category:
Ice-breaker

Aim

To help participants get to know each other, and to start disclosing at a simple level.

Issues raised by this exercise

Group dynamics.

Method

Hand each of the participants a questionnaire, having photocopied sufficient of the resource page for each person who will be taking part.

Ask them to pair off and find themselves a space in the room.

They have five minutes each to find out as much information as they can (or the other person wishes to reveal). After five minutes they should swap over and reverse roles.

When both questionnaires have been completed, you facilitate a round where each person is introduced to the group using the information in the questionnaire as a basis.

Anyone in the group may ask just one supplementary question of the person being introduced.

Feedback advice

This exercise is suitable for almost any type of course, and provides a non-threatening introduction for participants and helps to break the ice.

If you are running a course during which the importance of interpersonal relationships will be explored, you might capitalize on the exercise with some feedback to explore how the interviews actually went and what issues were raised.

RESOURCE PAGE

Interview pair questionnaire

Questionnaire

Name:

Age:

Place of birth:

What is the one thing you would most like to reveal to the group as a whole?

What is the funniest thing ever to happen to you?

What are your pet hates?

What are your interests outside of where you work or study?

What do you hope to get from this session?

Is there anything which is worrying you about this session?

Thank you for answering the questions.

28. Learning diary

Time guide: 30 minutes

Participants:
Whole group irrespective of size

Equipment and resources:
Flipchart or whiteboard; example of the learning diary review diagram which can then be copied onto the flipchart or whiteboard

Application:
Equal opportunities training
Staff development training
Management training
Interpersonal skills training
Assertiveness training
Quality of service training

Category:
Course closure

Aim

To provide a structured and comprehensive means of reviewing past learning, thereby encouraging students not only to learn through reflection but also providing them with a systematic mechanism for such review.

Issues raised by this exercise

Learning through reflection, structured feedback method.

Method

Explain the aim of the exercise to the students and identify a volunteer to lead the session. Encourage the leader to follow the review pattern for each learning point raised, by making good use of the learning diary diagram with its distinctive Y pattern. This pattern divides each learning point into the three categories:

What did we do?
How did we do it?
What learning did we get out it?

A good way of ensuring the group does not get lost is to encourage them to review a given part of the course in chronological sequence, referring to any timetables they may have been given at the start of the course.

It's a good idea to do a learning diary as an opening session reviewing the previous day.

Variations

You could lead the session rather than get a group member to do so if you think this is more appropriate for your learning group.

Feedback advice

This exercise is a form of feedback-generating activity which does not need to have a separate feedback phase included.

REVIEW DIAGRAM

Learning diary

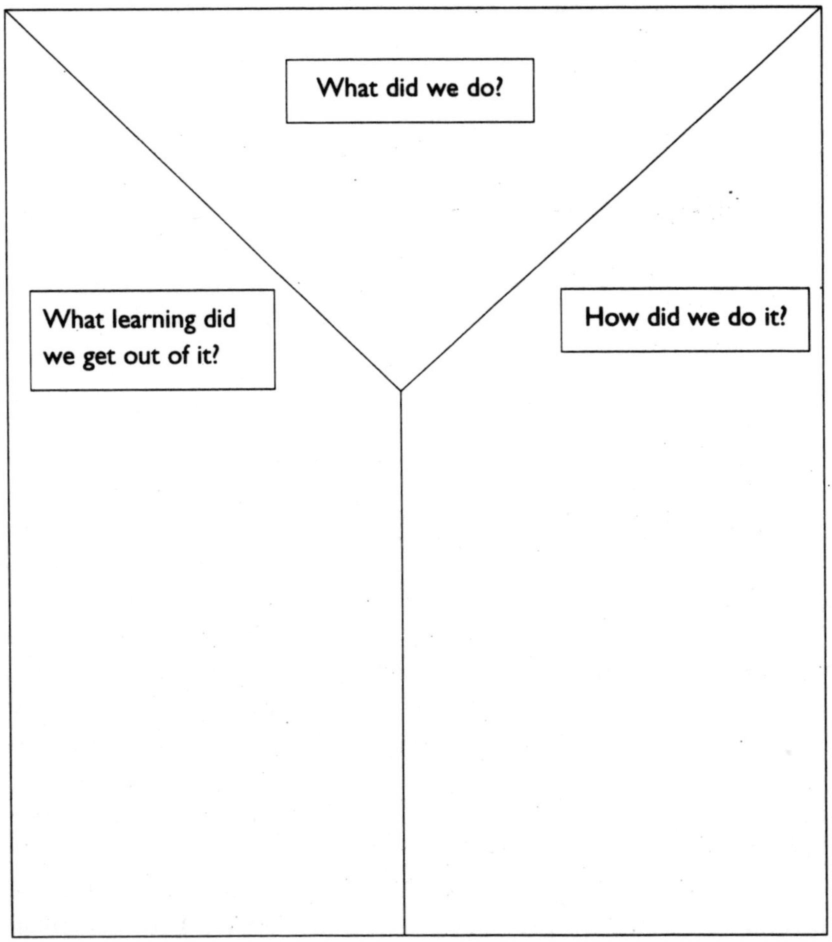

29. Management decision problem

Time guide: Half a day

Participants:
The exercise involves the active participation of six people, the rest of the group acting as observers

Equipment and resources:
The 'Management Decision Problem' package as provided in the resource page(s)

Application:
Management training
Interpersonal skills training
Assertiveness training
Quality of service training

Category:
Simulation

Aim

To encourage students to explore the skills involved in the management of conflict whether as a person who manages or as a person who is managed. Also the exercise will promote aspects of assertiveness and problem-solving which can be examined during feedback.

Issues raised by this exercise

The management of conflict, managing disappointment, management problem-solving, personnel management, assertiveness and communication skills.

Method

You should begin the exercise by briefing each role player separately, providing them with their role play sheet and clarifying together any misunderstandings. The observing group should also be briefed and tasked to watch the unfolding series of role plays with specific thought for the issues mentioned above. An observer sheet is provided to assist you in this task.

The first role play is between the two managers who will come together to discuss the problem and to review the workers' personnel outlines. It is for you to decide whether the workers should be allowed to observe this meeting or should be kept outside.

After the two managers have met, the interviews should follow during which each worker gets a chance to put their point of view.

Then, the two managers should again meet to review the interviews and make the decision.

Each worker should then be seen again by the managers to be told the decision, the reason for it and to enable the managers to try to allay disappointment and any sense of grievance.

Feedback advice

This is a long and complex simulation exercise requiring an effective, well-structured feedback session which draws heavily upon the findings of the observers while making full use of the role players' experiences. It is likely that the exercise will throw up too much material for a single feedback session and you must decide whether to capture the key learning and agree with the students that some things simply won't get covered, or allow more time to fully deal with the exercise effectively.

WORKER 1

Management decision problem

Background

You are a circuit builder in an electronics company and work in a small department along with five other people. You have two managers overseeing your work. One is a quality assurance manager and the other is the quality assurance deputy manager.

You are a good worker, punctual, hard-working and take pride in your work.

You have family living in Australia and they have recently offered you a holiday there. Although you knew the year's annual leave roster (used to book holidays) wasn't due out for a month, you nonetheless accepted and even bought your air ticket at a cost of £650.

The problem

It is now a week since the annual leave roster has been published and a row has erupted between all the staff in your sector, four of whom want the same two weeks off in the summer. The row has got so bad that the two managers have been asked by the senior management team to resolve the conflict.

Your viewpoint

You can understand that you jumped the gun by not waiting for the roster to be published but you now stand to lose £650 in cancelled air fare and a once-in-a-lifetime holiday in Australia. You don't think it would be right and fair to lose this opportunity just because of an administrative irregularity. You feel that you are probably the most reliable and hard-working person in the department and that this should count in your favour.

Approach when interviewed

You should remain calm, polite but assertive. Put your point of view across and emphasize your good work record. If asked about booking the holiday early, admit this error.

WORKER 2

Management decision problem

Background

You are a circuit builder in an electronics company and work in a small department along with five other people. You have two managers overseeing your work. One is a quality assurance manager and the other is the quality assurance deputy manager.

You plan to seek promotion in the company and to assist with your ambitions you are taking a course of study in your own time. You have exams due and desperately need to book two weeks holiday for study so as to be prepared for those exams.

The problem

It is now a week since the annual leave roster has been published and a row has erupted between all the staff in your sector, four of whom want the same two weeks off in the summer. The row has got so bad that the two managers have been asked by the senior management team to resolve the conflict.

Your viewpoint

You think that this is a management decision which should be taken with due regard to all the facts, including your position. After all, you are doing study in your own time with a view to advancement in the company and you feel this should count in your favour when a decision is made.

Approach when interviewed

You should remain calm, polite but assertive. Put your point of view across and emphasize your ambitions and commitment to the firm.

WORKER 3

Management decision problem

Background

You are a circuit builder in an electronics company and work in a small department along with five other people. You have two managers overseeing your work. One is a quality assurance manager and the other is the quality assurance deputy manager.

You are not the most punctual of people and would admit that at times your mind isn't always on your work but this is due to family problems which you are having to work through. Your mother, who lives with you and your husband, is ill and needs a lot of help and support; this is often in your thoughts and leads to you being late on the odd occasion.

Your mother is due in hospital for an important operation during the summer and you need two weeks off in the middle of the summer to help look after her when she is recovering at home. You have been told that these two weeks are heavily oversubscribed.

The problem

It is now a week since the annual leave roster has been published and a row has erupted between all the staff in your sector, four of whom want the same two weeks off in the summer. The row has got so bad that the two managers have been asked by the senior management team to resolve the conflict.

Your viewpoint

You are very worried about how you will come out of this issue and are concerned that your patchy work record may be misunderstood by management as laziness. You feel that you have a claim on these two weeks for personal reasons and that the firm should have a responsibility for its workers in such circumstances.

Approach when interviewed
You should remain calm, polite but assertive. Put your point of view across, explaining your predicament. Only justify your patchy work record if this is raised by the management. Raise the point about the company's personnel policy at such times.

WORKER 4

Management decision problem

Background

You are a circuit builder in an electronics company and work in a small department along with five other people. You have two managers overseeing your work. One is a quality assurance manager and the other is the quality assurance deputy manager.

You are a reasonably good worker, punctual and always do as you are asked but often no more.

You are the union representative for your section and became alarmed when a row broke about concerning annual leave during the summer. The company rule is that only two people from any section can take leave at the same time and this year four of the six people in your section want the same two weeks! You felt obliged to bring it to the attention of the managers and point out that one of your colleagues has tried to book a holiday early, which is against regulations.

The problem

It is now a week since the annual leave roster has been published and a row has erupted between all the staff in your sector, four of whom want the same two weeks off in the summer. The row has got so bad that the two managers have been asked by the senior management team to resolve the conflict.

Your viewpoint

You feel that as the union representative, a thankless task, you should have your claim dealt with before your colleagues', especially as you lost out in a similar conflict two years ago and were forced to take your holiday when you didn't want it. You feel it should be someone else's turn to lose their dates.

You feel very strongly and don't want to back down on this one.

Approach when interviewed

You should remain calm, polite but assertive. Put your point of view across explaining your past sacrifice and your current position, which you think should be in your favour.

QUALITY ASSURANCE MANAGER

Management decision problem

Background

You have been alerted by your senior management team that a problem has arisen in your section concerning holiday dates and that, apparently, four of the six workers in your section want the same two weeks off. This is against company policy (agreed with the union) which allows only two workers off at any one time.

You have just won a big new contract and this rule is more important than ever if you are to meet its deadlines. You have decided to meet with all four workers involved to find out what their position is before making the decision. You have also decided to enlist the help of your deputy at all stages.

Your task

You will be given personnel outlines on all four workers and you should first meet with your deputy to discuss each worker.

Your next move will be to undertake short interviews with each to ascertain what claim they feel they may have to these two weeks. These meetings will be run jointly by you and your deputy although you will take the lead.

You should then hold a further meeting with your deputy to make the decision.

Finally, again along with your deputy, you should speak with each worker in turn to inform them of the decision, your reasons for making it, and manage their disappointment.

DEPUTY QUALITY ASSURANCE MANAGER

Management decision problem

Background

You have been alerted by your boss that a problem has arisen in your section concerning holiday dates and that, apparently, four of the six workers in your section want the same two weeks off. This is against company policy (agreed with the union) which allows only two workers off at any one time.

You have just won a big new contract and this rule is more important than ever if you are to meet its deadlines. You have decided to meet with all four workers involved to find out what their position is before making the decision. Your help has been enlisted by your boss who would like your input at all stages.

Your task

You will be given personnel outlines on all four workers and you should first meet with your boss to discuss each worker.

Your next move will be to undertake short interviews with each to ascertain what claim they feel they may have to these two weeks. These meetings will be run jointly by you and your boss.

You should then hold a further meeting with your boss to make the decision.

Finally, with your boss, you should then speak with each worker in turn to inform them of the decision, your reasons for making it, and manage their disappointment.

PERSONNEL OUTLINE

Management decision problem

Worker 1
A good worker with an unblemished attendance record who takes pride in the work accomplished. Has never come to notice for any work or personal problems in the past. A circuit builder, as are all of those involved, with average experience, having been with the company three years. However, this worker did try to book a holiday before the holiday leave rosters were published, an arrangement which is against company policy.

Worker 2
A good worker who is clearly keen to get on and is prepared to take private study courses in order to advance in the company. Has never come to notice for any reason and has a good attendance record. Has been a circuit builder in the section for two and a half years.

Worker 3
This worker has a poor attendance record with occasional incidents of lateness and a tendency to lack concentration, leading to occasionally sub-standard work. Although no approach to personnel has been made by this worker, it is thought that domestic problems may be partially to blame for this patchy work record. Worker 3 has been a circuit builder in the section for three and a half years.

Worker 4
A fairly good worker who does what is required but never more than this. In fact, worker 4 is characterized by a work-to-the-rules attitude. That said, a

dependable and conscientious worker. This person is the union representative. The records show that worker 4 has previously been instructed to take a holiday at an off-peak time when a similar problem arose two years ago. Worker 4 was the person who brought the incident of early holiday booking by worker 1 to the attention of the management and was also the one who asked for management intervention in this conflict.

OBSERVER SHEET

Management decision problem

While you may not be directly involved in this exercise as a role player you nonetheless play a vital role as an observer and it is to you that the facilitator will turn when it comes time to feedback the exercise and uncover the learning which took place.

As you watch the role plays, think about the issues shown below and make notes of things which happen which relate to these issues. Pay particular attention to points from which you think the other members of the group will learn. Don't forget, it is very difficult when you are involved in role playing to grasp what is going on generally; as such, the role players will rely upon your observations for a lot of their learning.

Issues to watch out for

How is conflict managed?

What skills are being employed to arbitrate and conciliate or to secure compromise?

How fair are the managers being? Is there any sign of them favouring one candidate over another?

How assertive is each worker?

Does this assertiveness ever turn into aggressive or argumentative behaviour?

Are the managers able to minimize workers' disappointment through the way they deal with each person? If so, what skills are they employing? If not, why not, what's going wrong?

Would you have dealt with this situation differently, either as a worker but, more importantly, as a manager?

30. Me and my newspaper

Time guide: 30 minutes

Participants: Any size group

Equipment and resources:
A selection of newspapers of all types, tabloids and broadsheets – they do not have to be current; flipchart; broad nibbed pen; resource page

Application:
Equal opportunities training
Interpersonal skills training
Management training
Staff development training
Quality of service training

Category:
Encouraging learning through openness (attitudes, feelings)

Aim

To explore ways of thinking about attitudes and values and how these might be influenced by media images and slants.

Issues raised by this exercise

Attitudes, values, media influence and ways of thinking about issues.

Method

Announce that the purpose of the exercise is to explore our own ways of thinking, to see how others may think and to identify ways in which media images (in this case the press) may influence the way people think.

Divide the participants into smaller groups of three to work with each other

Issue each of the groups of three with a newspaper, ensuring a good balance between tabloids and broadsheets.

Issue each participant with the briefing sheet supplied as the resource page for this exercise, a piece of flipchart paper and a broad nibbed pen.

Each group now has 20 minutes to follow the instructions on the resource page. They should be prepared to share their findings with the larger group.

After the 20 minutes have expired, groups should post their flipchart sheet for all to see. Open the feedback by asking each of the groups to explain what they have put.

Feedback advice

This exercise can be tailored to suit all applications of training, because we are all to some degree influenced by the media, even if it is to have our own independence confirmed.

Your feedback therefore will need to focus on the area in which you are working, be it equal opportunities, management, personal development, or whatever.

Questions which will help you to get to grips with the issues raised by this exercise include:

'Is it true that we are influenced by the press?'
'Can we really tell how a person is likely to think and behave by the newspaper they choose to read?'
'Does our evidence suggest that newspapers really do take a particular stance?'
'In what ways might we be influenced ... subtly or overtly?'

RESOURCE PAGE

Me and my newspaper

You have been give a newspaper to work on.

On your flipchart (using lettering large enough for the whole group to see), please record the following information. In order to do so you will need to discuss with each other and search the newspaper carefully.

Name of newspaper

Editor

What political stance do you believe it to take?

What evidence for this can you find in the paper itself?

Give three examples of adverts in the paper

What type of readership do you think the advertisers are aiming at? Give evidence of this.

Give an example of the most salacious headline you can find.

What is the longest word you can find?

Would you read this paper regularly? Be prepared to say why or why not.

31. Mini-survey

Time guide: 1–1.5 hours

Participants: 15–20

Equipment and resources:
'Mini-survey' worksheet

Application:
Equal opportunities training
Staff development training
Management training
Interpersonal skills training
Assertiveness training
Quality of service training

Category:
Encouraging learning through openness (attitudes, feelings)
Course closure

Aim

To encourage students to take an active part in the process of group and individual disclosure in a lively and safe environment. This exercise also has the added benefit of encouraging greater learner autonomy by transferring the task of deciding at what level disclosure should be sought; this in turn will stimulate group commitment to that level of disclosure.

Issues raised by this exercise

The issues to be explored by the mini-survey can be chosen from key issues generated on the course to date. This ensures that opinions and attitudes canvassed will be relevant to the aims and planned learning outcomes of the course.

Method

You should explain the broad aim of the exercise to your students and emphasize how the structure enhances student autonomy through learner-directed decision making. You may wish to explain that it is for them to decide how probing and challenging the questions they design should be and as such it will be their choice as to what level of subsequent disclosure takes place.

In a quick plenary session, the group should agree the main topic they wish to explore, perhaps through brainstorming. This agreed subject will form the basis of question designing and the mini-survey itself.

After this initial and brief plenary session, students should be split into groups and tasked to design three questions to which they want answers from the larger learning group. The questions should focus on the agreed topic and should be written so that any response to the question can be in the form of:

strongly agree
agree
neither agree nor disagree
disagree
strongly disagree

Groups should be given the 'Mini-survey' worksheet which follows.

Once the worksheets are complete the survey can take place. This phase is fairly flexible and could be facilitator- or student-led; it can be run as a whole group session or by groups meeting up and taking turns to ask each other the questions on the worksheet that they have designed. Ultimately, you need to have a set of responses to each question which you can then use during evaluation of results and feedback.

Variations

You could gather all the worksheets up and, during a break, photocopy sufficient sheets to allow each student a chance to respond to all the questions created.

Feedback advice

The feedback really only comes into effect when student responses have been made and published. When this is done you can then discuss with the group the consequences of different responses and the attitudes they may uncover.

WORKSHEET

Mini-survey

Your task is to design three questions to which you as a group would like the reactions of your fellow students. The questions you design must be relevant to the topic you have agreed at the start of this session and should be designed in such a way that a respondent can answer by choosing from the five responses:

strongly agree
agree
neither agree nor disagree
disagree
strongly disagree.

It is up to you to decide just how challenging and probing these questions are going to be, but remember, if your questions are too shallow or bland they are unlikely to get any strong responses, whether agreement or disagreement.

QUESTION 1

Strongly agree *Agree* *Neither agree nor disagree* *Disagree* *Strongly disagree*

QUESTION 2

Strongly agree *Agree* *Neither agree nor disagree* *Disagree* *Strongly disagree*

QUESTION 3

Strongly agree *Agree* *Neither agree nor disagree* *Disagree* *Strongly disagree*

32. Nightmare scenarios

Time guide: 1 hour

Participants: Any size group

Equipment and resources:
Flipchart paper and broad nibbed pens, or whiteboard; resource page for this exercise

Application:
Equal opportunities training
Interpersonal skills training
Management training
Staff development training
Assertiveness training
Quality of service training

Category:
Simulation and/or role play
Encouraging learning through openness (attitudes, feelings)
Course closure

Aim

To enable learners to identify and confront situations which they find difficult to deal with.

Issues raised by this exercise

Assertive strategies, and living and operating in the real world.

Method

Introduce the aim of the exercise and stress that it is designed to encourage learners to identify the need and then generate their own ideas about how to deal with them. (*If you are involved in specific assertiveness training, this is a good exercise to use to practise assertive skills.*)

Issue the resource sheets for this exercise and then ask each student to work through the worksheet by detailing two nightmare scenarios and, where possible, strategies for resolving them. The resource sheet caters for each student to identify two scenarios.

It is important to realize that often the very problems and issues which students identify as nightmarish will be the ones they have most need to consider and work through. This is why this exercise is an excellent tool for identifying learning needs.

When all of your students have completed the worksheet as far as they feel they can, collect them in and collate the problems and issues identified, recording each scenario on a piece of flipchart paper.

Divide the learners into groups of three or four, distribute the flipchart evenly, and issue broad nibbed pens.

Each group should then be asked to generate as many resolution strategies or solutions to each of the scenarios as they can.

When this has been done, post the flipchart pages one at a time and facilitate a discussion of the implications.

Variations

This exercise can be used effectively to identify and confront difficult situations in most areas of training need. You can adapt it as needed to suit your own particular situation. For example we have found it to be very effective in training trainers to deliver equal opportunities training programmes. In such cases we usually ask the trainers to identify the questions they would least like to have to face from their learners.

Feedback advice

Be careful not to single out individual students with a view to identifying what their particular nightmare was.

Questions which will help to get to the issues include:

'How workable are the solutions offered for this nightmare?'
'Would this work in the real world?'
'If not, can we make any changes so the strategies would be workable?'

RESOURCE PAGE

Nightmare scenarios

My nightmare scenario is:	Possible coping strategies are:
My nightmare scenario is:	Possible coping strategies are:

33. Noticing non-verbals

Time guide: 1 hour

Participants: Any size group

Equipment and resources:
Resource page provided with this exercise

Application:
Equal opportunities training
Interpersonal skills training
Management training
Staff development training
Assertiveness training
Quality of service training

Category:
Simulation and/or role play
Encouraging learning through openness (attitudes, feelings)

Aim

To raise the learners' awareness of non-verbal communication and to develop skill in interpreting its meaning.

Issues raised by this exercise

Self-awareness, awareness of others, and communication.

Method

The exercise has three phases plus the feedback.

Phase 1

Announce the aim of the exercise, and explain that the purpose is to raise awareness of non-verbal behaviour and to practise interpreting it.

Ask the participants to pair off and sit together, facing each other.

For the next five minutes they should take it in turn to notice the non-verbal behaviour of the other person and say what they are seeing. They must not interpret at this stage. The other person stays silent. Change roles after five minutes and repeat the exercise.

Phase 2

Repeat the same as above but this time the person saying what they are seeing is allowed to make an interpretation; for example: 'I see you are rolling your eyes ... are you irritated with this exercise?'

The other person may non-verbally confirm or deny the correctness of the interpretation.

Phase 3

Issue each pair (change pairs if it seems appropriate) with the list of signals given as the resource page for this exercise.

Taking it in turns they are to communicate the signals on their list one by one, the partner trying to identify what is being communicated. After each signal the pair is to discuss what signals were received and what the sender thought was being sent.

Feedback advice

This exercise is suitable for all applications as the learning points relate equally in all contexts.

The stress of the feedback needs to be laid on two focal points:

1. Noticing the non-verbal behaviour. It is surprising how often we miss, or in many cases deliberately don't pick up on non-verbal cues given by people we are communicating with. This exercise helps to raise awareness of the signals we are constantly sent by others.
2. Interpreting what it means. The exercise also provides an opportunity to check with the sender whether a particular interpretation is correct.

Questions which may help to stimulate the feedback session include:

'How easy or difficult was the exercise?'
'Was it harder to notice the behaviour or to interpret it?'
'Who fell into the trap of interpreting the behaviour before noticing?'
'Why is it vital to pick up on non-verbal behaviour in a professional setting?'

RESOURCE PAGE

Noticing non-verbals

Lists of signals to communicate non-verbally:

Anger	Intrigue
Happiness	Superiority
Resignation	Piety
Sadness	Holier than thou
Boredom	Disinterested
Tiredness	Deception
Irritation	Disappointed
Non-cooperation	Smug
Resentment	Disagreement
Interest	Supercilious

34. Pass the conch

Time guide: 20–30 minutes

Participants:
Whole group (maximum 20)

Equipment and resources:
An object to represent the conch-shell. We have used a marker pen and a tennis ball in the past. Pick something small which can be handed or even gently thrown from one participant to the next

Application:
Equal opportunities training
Staff development training
Management training
Interpersonal skills training
Assertiveness training
Quality of service training

Category:
Ice-breaker
Energizer
Course closure

Aim

To give each group member the chance to contribute their ideas on a given topic in a quick and lively session.

Method

Get the group sitting in a circle and show them the object which is to represent the conch-shell. Explain that the holder of the conch has the chance of contributing on the topic being discussed for as long as they hold the conch. As soon as they have finished they should pass the conch to another member of the group.

You might start the session off as the holder of the conch and then pass it to a student, having provided an example of what you will expect students to contribute when they hold the conch.

A conch session could be a means of reviewing a course whereby the holder states briefly what they thought of the course and identifies some key learning to come out of it for them. Alternatively it could be used at the outset to identify fears or concerns the student may hold about the course.

Variations

Students can be given the opportunity to pass the conch to a particular student as a means of encouraging a response from that person.

Feedback advice

This is an active and dynamic session which is a form of ongoing and continual feedback on the topic being discussed. As such it should not need a separate feedback phase.

35. Quadrants

Time guide: 1 hour

Participants:
Needs a minimum of eight participants to be effective

Equipment and resources:
Resource page provided with this exercise; a room large enough to describe two bisecting lines as shown on the resource page

Application:
Equal opportunities training
Interpersonal skills training
Management training
Staff development training
Quality of service training

Category:
Encouraging learning through openness (attitudes, feelings)

Aim

For learners to orientate themselves in terms of attitudes and values, in relation to others and in relation to a set of criteria for a given issue.

Issues raised by this exercise

Values, attitudes, prejudice and discrimination.

Method

Announce the aim of the exercise, which is to find out (possibly literally) where participants stand on a given issue.

Clear away the chairs to leave ample space for the participants to work, then identify the four poles of the room which represent the most extreme positions on the issues to be worked through. You may want to do this in agreement with your students so that they feel comfortable with the issues to be worked through and the choice of positions which will become the four poles. (The resource page gives some ideas of the sorts of extreme positions you might describe.)

Once the poles have been described and any confusion or uncertainty resolved, ask the learners to stand in the position which most closely represents what they feel or believe to be where they stand in terms of their views, attitudes, beliefs, opinions, behaviour and so forth on the issues described. This will require some thought as they need to position themselves two-dimensionally!

When they are happy with their positions you can move among them and put questions to them about what their position and the position of other participants means to them. The feedback section for this exercise offers a number of suggested questions.

Variations

The exercise can be done on paper, ie, a flipchart if you and/or the participants prefer.

Feedback advice

As you move among the participants you should encourage disclosure (see Chapter 3) such as:

'Why did you choose this position?'
'Are you happy that you had to choose this position or would you like to move?'
'If you would like to move, what's stopping you?'
'If you do not wish to move, why is this?'
'How do you feel about the position of others?'
'How closely does your position match the values and ethos of your organization?'
'How does your position affect the job you do?'

RESOURCE PAGE

Quadrants

Suggested quadrants

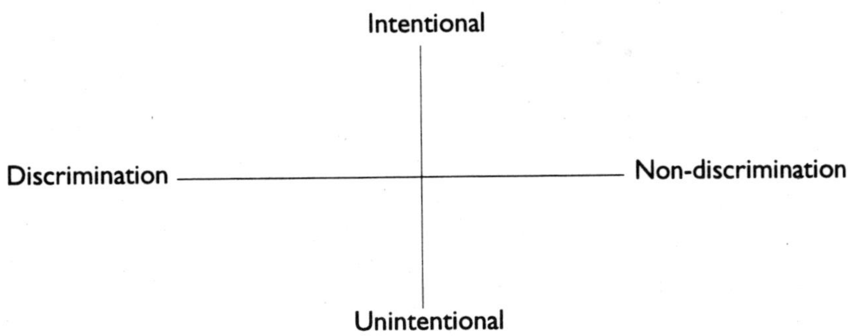

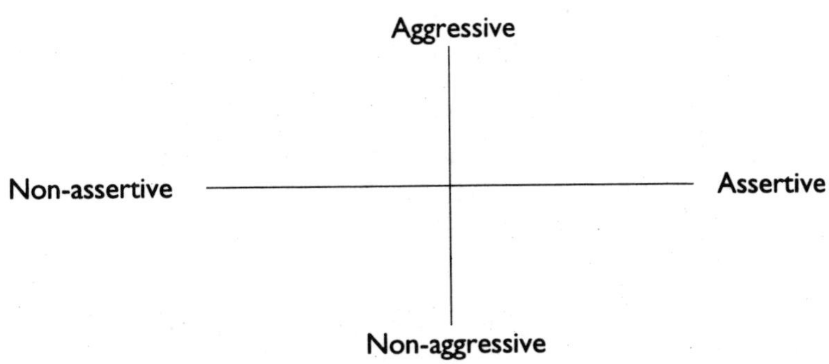

36. QUICK-FIRE BRAINSTORM

Time guide: 20–30 minutes

Participants:
Whole group, irrespective of size

Equipment and resources:
Either a flipchart and marker or whiteboard/chalkboard on which to record the results of the session

Application:
Equal opportunities training
Interpersonal skills training
Management training
Staff development training
Quality of service training

Category:
Energizer

Aim

To generate a large number of ideas on any given issue or problem in a lively and energetic manner in a short space of time.

Method

The facilitator explains the aim and emphasizes the pace and energy of the session, which should be kept short. Where possible the ideas (which should come thick and fast) should be noted down by a recorder, leaving the facilitator free to work with the group. It is important that the words and/or phrases offered by contributors should be recorded as said and without summarizing where possible. If a verbose contribution needs to be cut down, its final meaning should be agreed with the learner making the contribution.

The facilitator should emphasize that this is a brainstorming session and that all ideas are valid; choosing which ideas to work with will take place at a later time. The idea is to stimulate lots of points.

This method is difficult but not impossible without a recorder. The use of one or even two recorders will free the facilitator to work the group, maintaining a fast pace and keeping energy levels high.

Such a session need not be designed into a teaching plan but could easily be used 'off-the-cuff' to generate lots of ideas and perspectives.

Variations

Where there are co-facilitators working together the group could be split up into two separate groups.

Feedback advice

Once the ideas have been generated there will be a need to prioritize those which the group think are most relevant and/or pressing. This prioritization can be achieved by getting each group member to vote for points generated in the session which he or she would now like the group to work on. The simplest and most direct way of doing this is to encourage group members to tick the points on the flipchart they are voting for.

The number of issues the facilitator wants to focus on will suggest how many of the most popular issues will be chosen. For example, if the facilitator wants ten points to work on then the top ten can be 'lifted' from the main brainstorm and re-entered on a fresh flipchart or highlighted on the original.

37. Radical ideas Ltd

Time guide: 1.5–2 hours

Participants:
Whole group regardless of size

Equipment and resources:
This exercise will need a room large enough to allow each group to work unhindered by the other groups. Each group will need flipchart paper, marker and a number of 'Radical Ideas Ltd' worksheets

Application:
Management training
Interpersonal skills training
Quality of service training

Category:
Simulation

Aim

This exercise has three main aims:

1. To encourage students to examine the relationship between management structure, responsibility and decision making.
2. It will also encourage students to form and work within a team environment whereby individual ideas and decisions must be balanced with those of others.
3. The exercise will also test interpersonal skills as effective progress will depend upon good listening and communication skills

Issues raised by this exercise

Interpersonal skills, team building, decision making and problem-solving.

Method

You should explain the broad aims of the exercise to your students and hand out the worksheets which students should read and clarify as needed. It is important that you emphasize the need for teamwork and collaboration.

Split the group into a number of smaller groups such that each has about six or eight members. Make sure each group understands its task and has a flipchart and a marker or other appropriate writing materials. Arrange the room or rooms such that all groups can work comfortably without interference.

Start them working, informing them that they have about 40–45 minutes to complete the task and must address as many of the points given on the worksheet as they can effectively in the time allowed. They shouldn't rush to finish but nor should they get too bogged down on any single issue.

Feedback advice

A feedback sheet is provided as part of the resource pages for this exercise. You may want to undertake feedback on a small group basis (if you have a co-facilitator) although this is time-consuming! Alternatively, a plenary session should be set up. It is strongly recommended that students have a break between the exercise and the feedback.

You might find it useful to photocopy the questions on the feedback sheet and re-form students into their workgroups to think about their reactions to these questions before returning to plenary.

WORKSHEET

Radical Ideas Ltd

Background to the task

How many times have you heard people say things like, 'I could do what my boss does and probably do it better!' or, 'The management in this company is out of touch with the workforce' or how about, 'The management team in this company couldn't arrange a party in a brewery!' Well, if you have any sympathy with these sentiments or have ever thought you could do a better job than the people who manage you, this is your chance.

The task

You are a group of business people (all of whom are friends) who have come together to put into practice an idea you had some time ago. The idea was to build a completely and radically new type of company – not one based on hierarchical management but one with a totally new way of doing business.

The main role of the company will be to work with small inventors, bringing their ideas to life through your expertise in manufacture.

Your company will employ all sorts of people including administration clerks and secretaries, designers, project leaders, procurement managers, sales people, machine operators and others.

Your task is to construct a company structure which is in keeping with your company name, radical and different. How you design channels of responsibility and communication is up to you.

Within your design you must attempt to reach agreement in the following areas:

Decision making
Responsibility
Meetings
Wages, leave and perks
Hiring and firing

FEEDBACK SHEET

Radical Ideas Ltd

How difficult was the exercise?

What were the main problems encountered?

How difficult is it to align responsibility with position and reward?

What are the problems of having a flat management structure?

How well did the group work together?

Was there any conflict in the group and how was it resolved?

Did anyone take the lead and was their leadership helpful and accepted?

Did anyone feel they were shut out by others in the group?

Did anyone feel that their contributions were not valued by other group members?

38. THE RANGE EXERCISE

Time guide: 45 minutes–1 hour

Participants: Maximum 15–20

Equipment and resources:
A list of feedback questions and a list of examples, given on the resource pages; paper to make posters; a room large enough to allow students to stand in a line

Application:
Equal opportunities training
Interpersonal skills training
Management training
Staff development training
Quality of service training

Category:
Encouraging learning through openness (attitudes, feelings)

Aim

To encourage each student to reveal where they stand (literally) in respect of a given issue. It will also allow for student discovery of personal commitment towards change in opinion, attitudes and values and what might hinder this process of change

Issues raised by this exercise

The facilitator can decide which issue should be looked at and can then style the exercise accordingly (see method).

Method

Describe to your students or agree with them the issue which will form the focus of this exercise. Once decided, ask students to take a few minutes to quietly think about this issue for themselves.

While the students are thinking about the issue the facilitator should decide on two extreme positions which are relevant to the issue being worked on. For example, if the issue is about tolerance towards rude customers the two extremes might be, 'I am always totally tolerant towards rude customers' and, 'I am never tolerant towards rude customers' (remember this is just an example to give you an idea of how the exercise should be set up).

Using the 'Range Extremes' examples on the resource pages that follow, write each of your two extreme positions on a separate piece of paper and attach them to a wall or door with one poster opposite the other across the length of the room such that an imaginary line extends between them. This imaginary line represents the possible *range* of viewpoints between both extremes which become expressed by students in terms of the position on the line they adopt.

When the students are ready the facilitator should explain the layout of the exercise and read out the two extreme position posters, explaining that each student will be asked to stand on the imaginary line at a point between the two extreme poles which best represents where they stand on the issue. If two or more students want to occupy the same position on the line they should be allowed to stand side-by-side.

Variations

Students could be asked to discuss their relative positions on the line with those near to them.

Feedback advice

Feedback is best achieved with students standing in their positions on the range-line where they can be asked the questions listed on the feedback sheet included as one of the resource pages.

SOME EXAMPLES

Range exercise

Jokes which are racist are always wrong
Jokes which are racist are never wrong

Racism contained in humour and jokes is an important problem
Racism contained in humour and jokes is unimportant and never a problem

Racism is the fault of white people
Racism is the fault of black people

Minority ethnic groups should give up their cultural identity
Minority ethnic groups should retain their cultural identity

My behaviour is always sexist
My behaviour is never sexist

Good managers should always consult
Good managers should never consult

I always challenge rudeness in colleagues
I never challenge rudeness in colleagues

FEEDBACK QUESTION SHEET

Range exercise

Describe what your position on the range-line means to you.

Are you where you want to be in respect of this issue or would you prefer to be elsewhere on the range-line on this issue?

What is preventing you from moving to this new standpoint?

How realistic are the changes needed for you to be where you want to be on this issue?

What does the location of (identify another student elsewhere – probably some distance away) say to you about their views on this issue?

What are your views on the extreme positions chosen?

What are the consequences of your position for you and for others (bearing in mind that your position on the range line tells us your views on this issue)?

39. Reactions of others

Time guide: 45 minutes–1 hour

Participants: 15–20

Equipment and resources: Nil

Application:
Equal opportunities training
Staff development training
Management training
Interpersonal skills training
Assertiveness training
Quality of service training

Category:
Encouraging learning through openness (attitudes, feelings)
Role play
Course closure

Aim

To encourage students to think through the potential barriers to applying new learning, new ideas and new ways of thinking and behaving gained from the course in their own real world.

Issues raised by this exercise

The issues raised by this exercise will be dependent on the ideas raised by your students as they work through this exercise.

Method

Explain the broad aim of the exercise to your students, taking time to emphasize how important this phase of the course is to lasting learning.

On most facilitated courses, students are encouraged to develop new ways of thinking about issues, problems and experiences which confront them in their everyday lives. In the course of such learning, solutions, strategies and recipes for action are developed which, it is hoped, will be transferred to the real world outside the training setting. This exercise seeks to identify potential barriers to this application in order that students take a more realistic stance towards changing their behaviour and trying out what they have learned.

The initial phase is best done as a plenary session during which students are asked to contribute their thoughts on what barriers they may face in transferring the learning gained on the course to their real worlds. Their findings should be recorded on a flipchart or whiteboard.

The second phase can either be a general plenary discussion of these barriers and ways of overcoming them or, perhaps more effectively, a series of role plays during which students develop ways of overcoming barriers by facing them within the role play enactment.

We would suggest that solutions and strategies for overcoming barriers be recorded and students encouraged to make a note of those which are most relevant to them as individuals.

Feedback advice

Feedback as a distinct phase is largely unnecessary in this exercise and is probably best undertaken as ongoing facilitative guidance throughout the session.

40. Real-world role play

Time guide: 1 hour or more

Participants: Any size group

Equipment and resources:
Resource page provided with this exercise

> **Application:**
> Equal opportunities training
> Interpersonal skills training
> Management training
> Staff development training
> Quality of service training
>
> **Category:**
> Simulation and/or role play

Aim

To practise the skills and coping strategies required to deal with problems from the learners' real world.

Issues raised by this exercise

This exercise is one which is based entirely on the issues raised by participants in the group, so what is dealt with is variable.

Method

Phase 1

Announce the aim of the exercise and stress that the focus will be on the problems, issues and experiences that the learners have in their own real world.

The learners should then be asked to pair off and identify situations which they find difficult in their real world experience, and for which they would like to try out some coping strategies. The agenda for this can either be completely open or may, in part, be directed by you, if there are issues which you want the learners to particularly focus on.

Using the resource page for this exercise, they should then record these situations.

Phase 2

During this phase the learners will need to refer to phase 2 on the resource page. This gives clear instructions about what is expected of them but, as facilitator, you should be on hand to give advice and answer queries as necessary. Encourage your learners to improvise with props drawn from what is immediately available rather than anything elaborate. Too much realism can actually detract from the main focus which should be the experience, knowledge, skills and attitudes of the learners.

Phase 3

At this stage the pairs should be re-formed into new sets and the role plays performed. They can either be done one at a time in front of the group or simultaneously. The latter will save time, but has the drawback that some of the learning may be lost.

A useful feature is to ask them to swap roles so that the learners get a chance to see how another person might deal with the problem they have identified.

Phase 4

Feedback phase, advice for which is detailed below.

Feedback advice

Although the participants will get a great deal from the act of role playing their issues or watching their partner role playing, feedback will be important to gather together the learning and help distil some guidelines on how to cope in the future. Assuming you have familiarized yourself with some of the feedback advice given in Chapter 3, here are some questions which will help you maximize the learning from real-world role playing:

'Can you describe the scenarios which took place?'
'What was difficult?'
'What was easy?'
'What alternative strategies were used?'
'Which strategies worked best?'
'Did the partners deal with things in a different way?'
'Were any lessons drawn from that?'

RESOURCE PAGE

Real-world role play

Phase 1

Split into pairs and spend a few minutes talking over with your partner the things they find most difficult to do or say in terms of:

- challenging inappropriate behaviour
- dealing with difficult customers
- dealing with difficult colleagues
- any other situation which you avoid because you feel unable to cope with it.

Phase 2

Convert the situations you have identified into scenarios which you can work on and subsequently try out through role play. Make sure your scenarios:

- Have a clear aim – a statement of what problem, issue or experience you are trying to address.
- Are sufficiently detailed to enable a person who doesn't know anything about the situation to take part in the role play in a meaningful way.
- Contain briefings for the people involved in the scenario.

41. Round Robin

Time guide: 20 minutes minimum

Participants: Any size group

Equipment and resources:
Chairs arranged in a circle

Application:
Equal opportunities training
Interpersonal skills training
Management training
Staff development training
Quality of service training

Category:
Ice-breaker
Energizer
Course closure

Aim

To give an opportunity for every participant to speak about a given topic at a variety of depths.

Issues raised by this exercise

Depends on the purpose for which the Round Robin is used.

Method

Going round the group, members are asked to comment, say how they are feeling or give some other relevant information. For early stages of a course it would be usual to start with something simple, while part-way through or at the end of a course, the learners might be asked to comment in more depth about something. Here are some examples:

- *As an ice-breaker* – you might start with a round asking what participants do for a living, or what their hobbies are. This might progress to what they hope to get from the course and, finally, when they have had the opportunity to speak and loosen up, they might tell the group what they fear most about what will happen.

- *As a mid-course energizer* – you might do three rounds which start with what each participant has found funny so far, progresses to what has irritated them so far, and finishes with the direction they hope the course will now take.
- *As course closure* – you might do several rounds, allowing the participants an opportunity to say what they have got from the course, what they feel about the relationships that have built up and what they hope to do as a result of attending the training.

Variations

You could allow the learners to set the agenda for the Round Robin, getting them to identify the issues that will be disclosed.

Feedback advice

One of the main ways in which Round Robins are used is to allow space for participants to respond without any comment being made on what they have said. Feedback is therefore inappropriate for most Round Robins.

42. Selections

Time guide: One hour or more

Participants: A group of ten or more

Equipment and resources:
Resource pages supplied with this exercise; pair of dice

Application:
Equal opportunities training
Management training
(This exercise is most suitable for participants who have little or no knowledge of selection procedures, or the selection guidelines laid down by the Equal Opportunities Commission.)

Category:
Simulation/role play
Encouraging learning through openness (attitudes, feelings)

Aim

To identify valid criteria for advertising, selection and recruitment of people for particular occupations.

Issues raised by this exercise

Sexism, racism, prejudice and discrimination.

Method

Announce that the aim of the exercise is to draw up a list of criteria for people to be appointed to certain jobs.

Divide the participants into groups of three and issue each with a page of occupation lists (see the resource page) and a pair of dice or a calculator with a random button on it.

Allocate a different group of occupations to each set of three learners.

They choose their first occupation by rolling the dice (or using a random number selector on a calculator).

Their next task is to draw up a profile of the person they want to appoint for the job they have chosen. They do this by selecting one item from each of the 14 categories on the attributes list.

When each group has done this for three or more jobs, gather in plenary session and feedback.

Feedback advice

The main point of the feedback is of course to establish which criteria are relevant to the job and which have no bearing in the suitability of the person. Some participants may resent having been forced into making a choice (they certainly will if they have much experience of EO training), so be prepared for that. The feedback of this exercise assumes that you have a grounding in Equal Opportunities law and guidelines.

The following questions will help you get started in drawing out the learning:

'Which criteria are really necessary and which are not?'
'How did you decide which criteria to choose and which to reject?'
'Do you feel there is any element of stereotyping in your choice?'
'Did you draw upon your existing images of what a particular person in a particular occupation is like when thinking about criteria?'
'Can the choice of particular criteria tend to exclude parts of the population?'
'Are there any criteria which would indirectly discriminate against a particular group, even though they appear necessary?'
'Is there such a thing as women's work and men's work?'

ATTRIBUTES LIST

Selections

1. Age/Sex: 18–21, 22–25, 26–30, 31–40, 41–50, 51–65.
2. Colour: Black, White, Mixed Race, Yellow, Olive, Brown.
3. Ethnic background: British, Jewish, American, Scottish, Jamaican, Arab, French, Eurasian, Turkish, Welsh, Irish.
4. Education: Doctorate, Masters degree, Bachelors degree, A levels, O levels, GCSE, CSE, HNC, HND, BTech, professional qualification, no qualifications.
5. Religion: Catholic, Church of England, Muslim, Hindu, Buddhist, Jewish, Baptist, Methodist, Hare Krishna, Atheist, Agnostic, Swaminarayan, Jehovah's Witness.
6. Previous employment: unemployed, student, previous experience of job for which applying, previous relevant experience, career change, casual work, housewife.
7. Politics: Conservative, Labour, Liberal Democrat, Liberal, Green, Communist, Marxist, Socialist Workers Party, British National Party, National Front.
8. Hobbies: rock music, classical music, reading, watching television, computers, no hobbies, model-making, drinking, going out with the boys/girls, gardening.
9. Newspaper read: Times, Telegraph, Independent, Today, Sun, Mirror, Star, Caribbean Times, The Voice, Morning Star, Guardian, Sunday Sport.
10. Sporting interests: football, rugby, tennis, snooker, boxing, lacrosse, darts, running, athletics, canoeing, sailing, hang-gliding.
11. Strong beliefs (pro or anti): capital punishment, abortion, mixed mar-

riages, single-sex marriages, modern art, corporal punishment, school uniforms, sexual freedom, pornography, animal rights, censorship, gay rights, nudism, current licensing laws, freedom of speech, nuclear disarmament.

12. Qualities: reliable, punctual, honest, untruthful, diligent, sloppy, lazy, hard working, caring.
13. Personality: calm, sullen, reserved, pessimistic, moderate, severe, anxious, moody, quick tempered, restless, aggressive, excitable, changeable, impulsive, optimistic, active, tender, carefree, lively, easy-going, sensitive, talkative, sociable, even tempered, reliable, controlled, thoughtful, passive, cautious.

OCCUPATIONS LIST

Selections

Group 1

1. Accountant
2. Actor
3. Agricultural labourer
4. Airline pilot
5. Ambulance driver
6. Architect
7. Artist
8. Banker
9. Building labourer
10. Cook
11. Builder
12. Civil servant (low grade)

Group 2

1. Editor
2. Electrician
3. Engineer-electrical
4. Engineer-electronic
5. Engineer-civil
6. Estate agent
7. Film cameraman
8. Farmhand
9. Fireman
10. Forestry worker
11. Hotel chambermaid
12. Insurance salesman

Group 3

1. Nurse
2. Psychiatric nurse
3. Pharmacist
4. Photographer
5. Physiotherapist
6. Police officer
7. Politician
8. Printer
9. Public relations officer
10. Radio announcer
11. Waiter
12. Salesperson

Group 4

1. Clerical officer
2. Postal worker
3. Consultant
4. Data processor
5. Systems analyst
6. Designer
7. Dental nurse
8. Dentist
9. Doctor-GP
10. Doctor-surgeon
11. Driver
12. Economist

Group 5

1. Labourer
2. Lecturer
3. Librarian
4. Legal Executive
5. Lawyer
6. Judge
7. Magistrate
8. Musician-classical
9. Musician-rock
10. Mechanic-car
11. Reporter
12. Nursery nurse

Group 6

1. Research scientist
2. Secretary
3. Shop assistant
4. Stockbroker
5. Taxi-driver
6. Teacher
7. Youth worker
8. Charity worker
9. Milk delivery person
10. Refuse disposal worker
11. Telephone engineer
12. Athlete (full-time)

43. Sign-in exercise

Time guide: 30 minutes

Participants: Any size group

Equipment and resources:
Flipchart paper; broad nibbed pens; chairs arranged in a circle around the flipchart paper, which should be on the floor

Application:
Equal opportunities training
Interpersonal skills training
Management training
Staff development training
Quality of service training

Category:
Ice-breaker

Aim

To introduce the participants to each other and to encourage them to start speaking about themselves.

Issues raised by this exercise

Willingness to be open; group dynamics.

Method

Explain to the group that the purpose of the exercise is to encourage people to get to know each other and to get used to the idea, in a very non-threatening way, of revealing things about ourselves which might normally be hidden.

Place a piece of flipchart paper on the floor in the middle of the circle of chairs. Negotiate with the group what they would like to know about each other, and record a list of these things on a separate piece of flipchart, posted where all can see it.

Brief the group that in addition to the details on the flipchart, they should find an object in their pocket or bag which says something about them as a person. This could be a trivial item such as a cigarette lighter which says the person is a smoker, or more significant such as a diary, which says the person is busy and organized, or whatever.

The first person then moves over to the flipchart, crouches down and signs the flipchart (in the manner of the TV programme 'What's My Line?'). They can then return to their seat and tell the group the details about themselves which are listed on the posted flipchart. Finally they show the group their object and explain what it says about them as a person.

It would be a good idea for you, the facilitator, to go first to demonstrate the procedure.

Note: we believe that the act of getting up and crouching down (to sign the sheet) in front of the group plays an important role in helping the participant to loosen up and to relax the atmosphere.

Feedback advice

This exercise should achieve its aim with the minimum of feedback. If it appears, however, that some work does need to be done when the exercise is over, there are a number of avenues you could explore. Questions which might trigger such avenues include:

'Does a person's signature tell us anything about their personality?'
'Did anybody feel awkward about explaining their object?'
'Did anybody feel awkward about crouching down; if yes, why might this be?'
'Why does breaking the ice help learning?'

44. Strategy Meeting

Time guide: 3 hours approximately

Participants: 12–16

Equipment and resources:
Flipchart and marker for each group; 'Strategy Meeting' general information sheet included on the resource page

Application:
Equal opportunities training
Staff development training
Management training
Interpersonal skills training

Category:
Simulation

Aim

Within a team-building and collaborative situation this exercise seeks to encourage students to deal with various equal opportunities issues from a management point of view. As such it combines elements of interpersonal skills training, management training and equal opportunities training all within the one exercise.

Issues raised by this exercise

Sexual harassment, discriminatory behaviour, disability and sexuality, rights and equality, team building, inter-personal communication and the building of policy.

Method

You should carefully explain the broad aim and related issues raised to your students and then give each a 'Strategy Meeting' general information sheet. Allow students to read through the task sheet and clarify areas of confusion or difficulty.

Split the group into smaller groups of about six to eight people, ensuring that, as far as possible, each group can work without disturbing the other (a separate room for each would be ideal).

Provide each group with some flipchart paper and a marker pen or similar appropriate writing materials. Start the group working, explaining that they have about an hour to complete the task.

Carefully monitor the group, noting areas where they lack knowledge or display prejudice or attitudes which you might want to address later. Also keep an eye on general group dynamics and note learning points of an interpersonal nature as well, if desired.

If there is time you might like to consider a quick additional phase in which a spokesperson from each group is tasked to brief the other group on his/her own group's findings; this will allow all students to enter the feedback phase with knowledge of what the two groups came up with in response to the task sheet.

Feedback advice

As with any lengthy simulation, feedback needs to be carefully planned and structured so that as much effective learning can be drawn from the experience in the time available. Make full use of the notes you made while monitoring the group together with additional points arising from the publishing phase.

Areas where knowledge of equal opportunities legislation is weak or lacking should be dealt with.

GENERAL INFORMATION SHEET

Strategy meeting

Background to the problem

You are a member of the senior management team of a large corporation which employs several hundred people and part of your overall responsibility is to meet with other senior managers to decide company policy on key issues.

Recently, there have been a number of separate incidents amongst the workforce which although unconnected all fall within the area of equal opportunities problems. There have been a couple of cases of alleged sexual harassment, a gay man complaining that he is being victimized by colleagues, several female employees who are pregnant and want to know what the company plans to do in terms of structured maternity leave and return-to-work arrangements, and growing concern that a recent disabled applicant for a designer's job was turned down because of the cost of installing ramps and similar facilities to afford the person full access to the building.

The tasks in hand

There are two main tasks. The first is for the management team to design an equal opportunities strategy for the company which will have short- and long-term measures.

The second is to decide specific policy concerning two of the issues above, namely a policy on maternity and return-to-work measures for women employees, and to answer the question of recruiting and facilitating employees who have disabilities.

Other instructions

You should work as a team and record important decisions on a flipchart for future reference.

45. Tell me about

Time guide: 25–30 minutes

Participants: 15–20

Equipment and resources:
'Tell Me About' question sheet

Application:
Equal opportunities training
Staff development training
Management training
Interpersonal skills training
Assertiveness training
Quality of service training

Category:
Energizer
Encouraging learning through openness (attitudes, feelings)

Aim

To encourage an energetic and lively session of student disclosure in a safe learning environment, which can be designed to fit into the aim and planned learning outcomes of most types of facilitative courses.

Issues raised by this exercise

The issues raised by this exercise are determined by the headings included in the 'Tell Me About' question sheet, which can be amended to suit your own facilitative needs.

Method

You should outline the broad aim of the exercise and explain the lively nature of the session. The group should ideally be sitting in some form of circle or horseshoe configuration.

A student is selected at random and asked to pick a number between 1 and 30. This selected number will relate to a question on the question sheet. This number should be marked off in pencil (to prevent it being selected again by another student) and the student should be asked to tell the group about the topic shown at that number position on the question sheet. This is repeated with different students until the session is brought to a close.

Students should be asked to be as honest as they can and should be encouraged to respond without hesitation where possible.

Variations

If you feel that questions included in the example question sheet provided for this exercise are not relevant or appropriate for your group's learning needs, you can simply insert a different topic of your own choosing.

Feedback advice

As students respond to the questions asked, points which you feel should be addressed further should be noted and discussed during a feedback session following the exercise.

QUESTION SHEET

Tell me about

Students should be asked to pick a number between 1 and 30 and, depending on the number they choose, should be asked to tell the group about the subject which corresponds to that number. Once a number has been picked, a mark should be made against it in pencil so that it cannot be selected again by another student.

1. Black culture
2. Feminism
3. Gypsies
4. Sex Discrimination Act
5. Race Relations Act
6. Vicarious liability
7. Communication with people who are deaf or have hearing impairment
8. Being white
9. Racism today
10. Employment and pregnancy
11. Age of consent for gay men
12. Good listening
13. Being assertive
14. Dealing with conflict
15. Attitudes you hold which you'd like to change
16. Attitudes others hold which you don't like
17. Immigration
18. Positive action
19. Good management techniques
20. Bad management techniques
21. Empathy
22. Sexual harassment
23. Wheelchair users
24. Your culture
25. Asian culture
26. The saying, 'Man's work'
27. The saying, 'It's a man world'
28. Gay rights
29. Non-verbal communication
30. A prejudice you hold

46. THREE WISHES

Time guide:
2 minutes for each participant

Participants: Any size group

Equipment and resources: Nil

Application:
Equal opportunities training
Interpersonal skills training
Management training
Staff development training
Quality of service training

Category:
Ice-breaker
Energizer
Encouraging learning through openness (attitudes, feelings)

Aim

To encourage participants to speak and be open in the group in a way which is completely non-threatening.

Issues raised by this exercise

Willingness to share feelings and personal information with the group; values clarification.

Method

Participants sit in a circle.

Announce the aim of the exercise and explain that each participant should think for a moment about three wishes they would make:

'One thing they wish had not happened to them in the last week.'
'One thing they wish had happened to them in the last week.'
'One thing they wish they could take away from the course/seminar.'

Variation

Bear in mind the need to adapt as necessary to the real-world experience of your learners. You might, for example adapt the wish to:

'One thing you wish would change in your workplace.'

Other variations depend to a large extent on the category the exercise is being used in. If you are using it as an ice-breaker or energizer, then you will probably not need any feedback at all. If you have selected the exercise to encourage, say, non-assertive participants to speak and explore how it feels to be sharing with the group, then feedback will certainly be necessary.

Feedback advice

While this exercise can be as superficial or as penetrating as you wish, you should be prepared for responses which are unexpected or which will need sensitive handling. For example, we once experienced a participant whose wish for a relative (who was seriously ill) moved her and others in the group to tears. By the same token, it is equally possible that the session will generate humour, with someone wishing that something funny had not happened to them. Your own approach will set the mood.

If you are using the exercise to encourage learning through openness, the following questions may be useful:

'How easy/hard was it to reveal your wishes to the group?'
'Did anyone have things they wanted to say but felt they couldn't? Why might this have been?'

47. Torpedo

Time guide: 40 minutes

Participants: Any size group above six

Equipment and resources:
At least four sheets of flipchart paper, each headed as follows:

'One thing I bring to the course'
'One thing I want to take away from the course'
'One thing I could do to ensure the group will not achieve its aim'
'One thing I could do to ensure I will not meet my aim';

four broad nibbed pens; tape to stick flipchart paper to wall; briefing sheets for participants, provided as the resource page for this exercise

Application:
Equal opportunities training
Interpersonal skills training
Management training
Staff development training
Quality of service training

Category:
Energizer
Encouraging learning through openness (attitudes, feelings)
Course closure

Aims

1. To help participants clarify their expectations and concerns of a seminar and the potential obstacles to success.
2. To provide a checklist for action planning at course closure.

Issues raised by this exercise

Group dynamics, personal expectations and group expectations.

Method

Announce the aim of the exercise and issue each participant with a briefing sheet on which to record their ideas. The sheets are important because they will also be used at the end of the course to check on progress and provide a suitable vehicle for making a personal action plan.

After about seven to ten minutes, when the briefing sheets have been completed, ask the participants to visit each area of the room where you will by now have posted the pre-headed flipchart. Ask them to write a one-line summary on each sheet. These will be used as a guide throughout the course to help keep things on track and to identify whether people are actually implementing what it is they said they could do to make progress.

Variations

The exercise can also be used as a check on progress halfway through a course or at a suitable point such as after lunch.

The title of the sheets can also be changed to suit the purpose of your course.

Feedback advice

When each participant has finished putting up their contributions, post the sheets for all to see, and then do several rounds of the group asking the participants to take ownership of them and amplify them if they wish. You may well find that this area of the discussion starts to expand into the core business of your course. It will be for you to decide in consultation with the participants whether you wish to pursue the issues at this stage.

RESOURCE PAGE

Torpedo

One thing I bring to the course:

One thing I want to take away from the course:

One thing I could do to ensure the group will not meet its aim:

One thing I could do to ensure I will not meet my aim:

48. TURNING THE TABLES

Time guide: 45 minutes

Participants: 12–15

Equipment and resources:
'Turning the Tables' worksheet

Application:
Equal opportunities training
Staff development training
Management training
Interpersonal skills training
Assertiveness training
Quality of service training

Category:
Encouraging learning through openness (attitudes, feelings)

Aim

To encourage students to explore potential ways of dealing with problematic situations or people through role-reversal.

Issues raised by this exercise

The issues dealt with in this exercise depend on what each participant identifies as a learning need during the initial reflection phase of the exercise

Method

Initially you should explain the aim of this exercise and hand each student a 'Turn the Tables' worksheet which they should be asked to read thoroughly. You should check with the group that the instructions contained within the worksheet are readily understandable and achievable.

Working alone, each student should then work through the task sheet which requires the construction of a simple short scenario role play. In the role play the student will take on the part of the person whom, in real life, they have problems dealing with in an appropriate or effective manner. This difficulty could arise for any reason, whether through a lack of assertiveness, embarrassment, lack of empathy or sensitivity or lack of control, and this should be explained to students at the outset.

The next phase, having decided which role play the group will focus on, involves the student who designed it briefing the group about the scenario and providing instructions to others who will take on allotted roles. Often these simple role-reversal role plays will involve only two people, the student (played by another person) and the individual who is the source of the problem played by the role play designer.

This exercise allows the student not only the chance to try and get inside this problematic other person but also a chance for them to look back at themselves from the point of view of that other person. This should be explained during the feedback session.

It is essential that the person who is tasked to role play the student understands the types of responses that are typical of their past encounters together, as this will increase the authenticity of the experience.

Variations

The student could try on both parts in the same role play in an attempt to get a full idea of what's going on.

Feedback advice

This can prove a fairly emotive session and requires careful, sensitive and supportive facilitation. If you feel that the role reversal is moving into areas which will prove difficult to feedback adequately, manage the session to avoid this by directing the group as necessary. Don't be afraid to encourage observers to offer advice or ideas about what they think is going on in the encounter or the way in which they would handle it. Even spontaneous role play to illustrate alternative recipes of action may prove appropriate and illustrative.

WORKSHEET

Turning the tables

All of us have had encounters with people who, on reflection, we found difficulty dealing with effectively. Maybe the person manages to irritate us, or maybe their behaviour overpowers us and we cannot summon up assertive responses. Alternatively, it may be that we dealt badly with the situation, being insensitive or intolerant.

The purpose of this session is to give you the chance to role reverse. This means you get to be that other person and another student, briefed by you, gets to play you! This will give you the chance to really get inside this other person's character and at the same time see yourself from that person's point of view.

Your initial task, then, is to think of a typical scenario where, in an encounter with this person, you almost invariably get into problems. Keep it simple and try to design this role play so as to involve as few people as possible; this will make it quicker and easier to run and less complicated.

Make sure you note down what each person has to do in your role play. When it's your turn to lead the session you will be asked to explain your role play to the group and then to brief the other role players who will help you. What is vitally important is that you carefully instruct the student who is to play you about the way you normally behave in this typical situation; that way the role play will be as authentic as possible.

49. WHAT DO YOU *REALLY* THINK ABOUT . . . ?

Time guide: 1 hour

Participants: Group of 10 or more

Equipment and resources:
Resource sheet provided with this exercise, with sections cut up and pasted onto postcard size card; use your own sections if you are opting for the variation

Application:
Equal opportunities training
Interpersonal skills training
Management training
Staff development training
Quality of service training

Category:
Energizer
Encouraging learning through openness (attitudes, feelings)

Aim

To encourage participants to be open about/discover what they really think about issues.

Issues raised by this exercise

Prejudice, stereotyping, labelling, attitudes, and values clarification.

Method

This exercise relies on the quick-fire nature of the transactions of the participants to make it successful.

Announce the aim of the exercise.

Give each participant one or more of the issue cards you have made from the resource page.

Instruct the participants to circulate in the room.

Using the card(s) they have been given, they are to go up to each other and ask 'What do you *really* think about . . . (whatever is on the card)'.

The person to whom the question is put should give an immediate off-the-cuff reply, and it should be received by the questioner without comment, and certainly without any judgement.

Participants continue to circulate until they have put all the questions to each other.

Variation

Variations for this exercise will largely depend on the subject area in which you are working. The examples we have given as the resource page fit most neatly in an equal opportunities/fair treatment training programme. Having said that, you can adapt them as necessary to help participants focus on specific areas which may be of concern to your programme. Some other ideas are given below.

Quality of service training
'What do you *really* think about...?'

Customers	Clean shoes
Mission statements	Being polite
The Citizens Charter	The customer is always right
Professionalism	The customer's need to know
Punctuality	

Management Training
'What do you *really* think about...?

Teams	Citizens charters
Target setting	Leadership
Performance related pay	Consultative management styles
Competitive tendering	Counselling
Local management of budgets	Stress in managers

Feedback advice

This exercise will generate a great deal of learning between the participants while it is actually in progress. Having said that, there will be a great deal more learning to be unearthed with good feedback afterwards.

It is probably a good idea to start with a round to ask each participant to say a few words about their own reaction to the exercise. After that you can begin to work with some of the content of what was said. If people say that they didn't really think anything about a particular issue, it might raise the issue that adopting a neutral attitude is actually putting one's head in the sand. Some questions that will help to stimulate the learner's thinking include:

'Was anybody surprised by the way they answered any of the questions?'
'Was anyone surprised by any of the answers they received?'
'How far do you think what was heard represented real views and why?'
'Were there any specific issues raised which could help us understand the process of labelling/stereotyping/our attitudes or values?'
'When we respond to issues in the real world, we often react instinctively rather than in a cold reasoned way; do you think this is true?'

RESOURCE PAGE

What do you *really* think about . . . ?

Homosexuality	Muslims	Buddhists	The welfare state	Racism
Racist jokes	The British Movement	The homeless	Hindus	Equality for all
Giving everyone a level playing field	Prejudice which is personal	Skinheads	EO policy statements	Immigration
Women who work	Travellers	Black people	Political correctness	People in wheelchairs
Positive action programmes	Gypsies	New Age travellers	Council housing	People who live in large houses
Gay people	Sexist humour	Christians	The Irish	Repatriation

50. Who Said What and Why

Time guide: 30–45 minutes

Participants: 15–20

Equipment and resources:
'Who Said What and Why' hopes and fears cards provided as resource page

Application:
Equal opportunities training
Staff development training
Management training
Interpersonal skills training
Assertiveness training
Quality of service training

Category:
Ice-breaker
Energizer

Aim

To encourage each student to identify their individual hopes and fears concerning the course and to explain these to other members of the group in a phase which seeks to encourage interaction between students who may have not met each other before.

Issues raised by this exercise

Interpersonal interaction.

Method

Explain the aim of the exercise to your students and distribute each with two 'hopes' cards and two 'fears' cards. Tell the group that the first phase requires them to think individually about the course they are about to become involved in and then to identify any concerns or expectations they may hold. Each student should then write up to two hopes and two fears on the cards provided.

These cards are then shuffled and distributed to the group so that *no* person ends up with a card of their own. Students then mingle and attempt to match the cards they hold with the people who wrote them. Every time a student 'meets' someone and asks them whether they are the author of any cards the student is holding, each should also introduce themselves to the other person.

Should a student match a person with a card, they should seek to discover why that person holds a specific concern or expectation about the course. The session should continue until everyone has found their corresponding partners or the time allotted to the exercise runs out.

Feedback advice

A plenary session should be considered, if time allows, during which all the hopes and fears disclosed become recorded and discussed within the group. Where useful, concerns can become linked with group rules (see the exercise Group Rules).

RESOURCE PAGE

Who said what and why

I hope that this course will . . .	I hope that this course will . . .	I am concerned that this course . . .	I am concerned that this course . . .
I hope that this course will . . .	I hope that this course will . . .	I am concerned that this course . . .	I am concerned that this course . . .
I hope that this course will . . .	I hope that this course will . . .	I am concerned that this course . . .	I am concerned that this course . . .

Part III

Matrices and Index

MATRIX 1: EXERCISE TYPE LOCATOR

EXERCISE TYPE LOCATOR

		Page	Ice-Breaker	Energizer	Encouraging Learning....	Simulation/Role Play	Course Closure
1	Agreeing the Issues	53			●		
2	Anonymous Disclosure	56			●		
3	Are You Being Served?	60			●		●
4	Attitude Ballot	64			●		
5	Behaviour Arrays	70				●	
6	Best Laid Plans	72					●
7	Best Manager	76			●		
8	Beyond Disclosure	79			●		
9	Birthdays	83	●	●			
10	The Black Cat Exercise	85		●			
11	Bust that Myth!	88			●	●	
12	Challenge Escalation	94			●	●	
13	Challenge Identification	98			●	●	
14	Characteristics of a Support Person	102			●		●
15	Consequences	106			●		
16	Constructing Stereotypes	109			●		
17	Cultural Objects	112			●		
18	Draw What You Think	115		●	●		
19	Faulty Goods	118			●	●	
20	Find Someone Who....	121	●	●			
21	Future Action Challenge	125					●
22	Group Rules Exercise	128	●		●		
23	Identify the Language	131			●		
24	'I'm Like This and You're Like This'	134			●		
25	Inappropriate Attitudes and Behaviour	138			●		
26	In-group, Out-group	141			●		
27	Interview Pair Questionnaire	145	●				
28	Learning Diary	149					●
29	Management Decision Problem	152				●	
30	Me and My Newspaper	166			●		
31	Mini-Survey	170			●		●
32	Nightmare Scenarios	173			●	●	●
33	Noticing Non-verbals	176			●	●	
34	Pass the Conch	179	●	●			●
35	Quadrants	181			●		
36	Quick-Fire Brainstorm	184		●			
37	Radical Ideas Ltd	186				●	
38	The Range Exercise	190			●		
39	Reactions of Others	194			●	●	●
40	Real-world Role Play	196				●	
41	Round Robin	199	●	●			●
42	Selections	201			●	●	
43	Sign-in Exercise	206	●				
44	Strategy Meeting	208				●	
45	Tell Me About	211		●	●		
46	Three Wishes	214	●	●	●		
47	Torpedo	216		●	●		●
48	Turning the Tables	219			●		
49	What Do You *Really* Think About...?	222		●	●		
50	Who Said What and Why	226	●	●			

MATRIX 2: EXERCISE APPLICATION LOCATOR

EXERCISE APPLICATION LOCATOR

		Page	Equal Opportunities Trng	Staff Development Trng	Management Trng	Interpersonal Skills Trng	Assertivenes Trng	Quality of Service Trng
1	Agreeing the Issues	53	●	●	●	●	●	●
2	Anonymous Disclosure	56	●	●	●	●	●	●
3	Are You Being Served?	60	●	●	●	●		●
4	Attitude Ballot	64	●					
5	Behaviour Arrays	70	●	●	●	●	●	●
6	Best Laid Plans	72	●	●	●	●	●	●
7	Best Manager	76			●	●		●
8	Beyond Disclosure	79	●	●	●	●	●	●
9	Birthdays	83	●	●	●	●		●
10	The Black Cat Exercise	85		●	●	●		●
11	Bust that Myth!	88	●	●		●	●	
12	Challenge Escalation	94	●	●	●	●	●	●
13	Challenge Identification	98	●	●	●	●		
14	Characteristics of a Support Person	102	●	●	●	●	●	●
15	Consequences	106	●	●	●			●
16	Constructing Stereotypes	109	●	●	●	●		●
17	Cultural Objects	112	●					●
18	Draw What You Think	115	●	●	●	●		●
19	Faulty Goods	118		●	●	●	●	●
20	Find Someone Who....	121	●	●	●	●	●	●
21	Future Action Challenge	125	●	●	●	●	●	●
22	Group Rules Exercise	128	●	●	●	●		●
23	Identify the Language	131	●	●	●	●		●
24	'I'm Like This and You're Like This'	134		●	●	●		●
25	Inappropriate Attitudes and Behaviour	138	●					
26	In-group, Out-group	141	●					
27	Interview Pair Questionnaire	145	●	●	●	●		●
28	Learning Diary	149	●	●	●	●	●	●
29	Management Decision Problem	152			●	●	●	●
30	Me and My Newspaper	166	●	●	●	●		●
31	Mini-Survey	170	●	●	●	●	●	●
32	Nightmare Scenarios	173	●	●	●	●	●	●
33	Noticing Non-verbals	176	●	●	●	●	●	●
34	Pass the Conch	179	●	●	●	●	●	●
35	Quadrants	181	●	●	●	●		●
36	Quick-Fire Brainstorm	184	●	●	●	●		●
37	Radical Ideas Ltd	186			●	●		●
38	The Range Exercise	190	●	●	●	●		●
39	Reactions of Others	194	●	●	●	●	●	●
40	Real-world Role Play	196	●	●	●	●		●
41	Round Robin	199	●	●	●	●		●
42	Selections	201	●		●			
43	Sign-in Exercise	206	●	●	●	●		●
44	Strategy Meeting	208	●	●	●	●		
45	Tell Me About	211	●	●	●	●	●	●
46	Three Wishes	214	●	●	●	●		●
47	Torpedo	216	●	●	●	●		●
48	Turning the Tables	219	●	●	●	●	●	●
49	What Do You *Really* Think About...?	222	●	●	●	●		●
50	Who Said What and Why	226	●	●	●	●	●	●

Index